1125 Harvard East

KAY BULLITT'S GATHERING PLACE

*It is a gracious house
and ever was friendly to
strangers and a home to friends*

*The God of heaven's music loved
this place."*

— Above Kay Bullitt's fireplace
from Euripides' *Alcestis*

1125 Harvard East

KAY BULLITT'S GATHERING PLACE

Sam R. Sperry

1125 Harvard East: Kay Bullitt's Gathering Place
By Sam R. Sperry

Copyright © 2014 by Sam R. Sperry and Kay Bullitt

Expanded Edition, May 2014

Editing by Barbara Spaeth
Design by Nancy Kinnear
Index and proofreading by Miriam Bulmer

ISBN: 978-0-9794193-1-7

1. Bullitt, Katharine Squire Muller, 1925– . 2. Civic leaders—
Seattle (Washington)—Biography.

Printed in Seattle by Consolidated Press

To Winnie.

When you bring people together

around a purpose,

good things happen.

— Kay Bullitt

Contents

Preface

The call from Dorothy inquired whether I might know of someone, preferably a journalist, who might be interested in doing "a book on my mother's house." She explained that during the nearly 60 years Kay Bullitt has lived there, an enormous and varied catalog of events had taken place inside and outside in the big yard. Many people (some well known, some not) had come by, been married, been memorialized, benefited from fundraising parties, enjoyed and made music, talked politics, experienced joy and sorrow of personal and family celebrations and losses, or had simply come over to visit.

I had known Dorothy since the late 1980s, having met her in my capacity as a member of the *Seattle Post-Intelligencer* editorial board. Later, we would work together: she as executive director of the Seattle-South King County Chapter of Habitat for Humanity; me as a member of the chapter's board of directors. Dorothy and I shared similar interests, attitudes and political preferences. But I had never met Kay Bullitt.

As we talked about the book, that Kay wanted to relate her life's work as educator, civic activist, peace advocate, historic preservationist, supporter of the arts, loyal Democrat, mother and friend, in a form that would be meaningful to her grandchildren, I warmed to the assignment. Would they consider me, me who for years had sworn I would never write a book? Yes, they would.

I knew of Kay. She had appeared from time to time before the Seattle City Council to offer testimony on one subject or another. I covered City Hall in the early '70s for *The Seattle Times*. One does not forget Kay's presence: her dazzling plume of white hair, her intelligence, her poise, her efficient speech. But I had never met her. "Dorothy, I'd better meet your mom to be sure she wants me to take this on." Dorothy agreed.

A challenge for this project would be how to relate Kay's activities over a 60-year span of time for people born in the '80s and '90s — most particularly her grandchildren. The changes in Seattle, King County and Washington state during those years have been dramatic. To tell this story properly would require laying a foundation of what things were like in Seattle after World War II, in the 1950s, providing contexts for the many endeavors and works Kay sponsored and participated in, and tapping the memories of at least some of the key players and personalities who had joined with her in the variety of activities she pursued.

I presented Kay with a rough outline of what this book might be like: two major story arcs: her civic/political work and the personal, family life of wife, mother and friend. We agreed on this. Dorothy had cautioned me that Kay's well-filled files — more than 100 boxes — plus her résumé, five pages long, is top-to-bottom full with single lines, each enumerating a different activity.

"You mustn't let the perfect become the enemy of the good," she said, firmly. Sage advice.

What follows is a biographical story, Kay's story, not a biography. For this story we have selected about 35 activities, events and episodes from Kay's life. Some necessarily receive more detail than others. Some require more backgrounding and context than others. Some activities and events flow and evolve and grow as Kay's life evolves. Others are more one-off episodes. So saying, they all congeal into a narrative.

For what it's worth, this Seattle kid, who grew up here, whose first experience with television was watching Mrs. Dorothy Stimson Bullitt on Thanksgiving Day throw the switch to light up King Broadcasting's tower on Queen Anne Hill, who is a history-politics addict — and, truth be told, who has long admired the Bullitt family for the immense good they have wrought and continue to sponsor in our community — who met his bride here and who helped raise his family here, the opportunity to write about Kay Bullitt and what she has done and continues to do here, and about his hometown, was just too good to pass up.

Overture

IT WAS A BRISK BUT CLEAR MARCH DAY, NOT THAT THE WEATHER
MATTERED TO KAY AND STIM. THEY WALKED AROUND THE
LARGE, LUSH-GREEN PROPERTY AT 1125 HARVARD AVENUE EAST,
SURVEYING THE IMMENSE ELM, THE MAJESTIC CEDAR, AND THE
VINE MAPLE AND BIRCH TREES THAT DOMINATED THE SPACE. THE
LOT EXUDED A FRESH, QUIET, PEACEFUL AMBIENCE. IT WAS QUITE
A SPOT INDEED.

Situated on the western crest of Capitol Hill in one of Seattle's
loveliest and oldest neighborhoods, the spacious property overlooked Lake Union to the northwest, out toward Puget Sound to the
west, and then southwest to the Denny Regrade. It was long before
the Space Needle punctuated the city's skyline.

The trees and an array of shrubs made for a park-like setting.
The large grassy yard was flat until it sloped off to the west, down
to a brick wall abutting the properties below on Boylston Avenue

East. There was plenty of room for play, plenty of spots to sit and enjoy a quiet repose.

Stim asked Kay to marry him. She accepted.

Stim said he would build a house for them on the site. Kay thought that was a wonderful idea. She loved the neighborhood. The spacious property, an acre and three-quarters, would be ideal for raising a family and hosting parties and other events. She had been in Seattle only a year. She thought the city held a lot of promise. Now she was putting down real roots.

It was 1954. Seattle was a very different place then. Together and separately, Kay and Stim Bullitt would play important roles in what Seattle would become. And so this story begins.

A passenger vessel approaches the central
Seattle waterfront in the mid-1950s.

Chapter 1

Provincial but promising: Seattle in the 1950s

In social terms, Seattle was
"white bread," steady and solid,
a good place to raise a family
— especially if you were white.

Arriving

It may seem harsh now, but the Seattle Kay Muller encountered when arriving in 1953 was every bit Northwest provincial. A placid, middle-class city of medium size, a beautiful place surrounded by water, Seattle then was rather unexciting, but for its natural beauty.

The city rose on seven hills astride one of North America's most perfect harbors, sheltered Elliott Bay, deep enough for large freighters, scenic and inviting. Puget Sound provided its western border, 26-mile-long Lake Washington its eastern. On a clear day, one could view the magnificent Cascade Mountains beyond the lake, and southeasterly the majestic, imposing Mount Rainier. To the west

Fanfare Sets Cars Rolling Along Span

By ROBERT HEILMAN

They snipped the ribbon on the Alaskan Way Viaduct yesterday afternoon — singing and dancing and playing music and jumping up and down and snapping pictures and gesturing and making impassioned speeches.

Eight mililon dollars' worth of overhead highway construction suddenly came into its own.

Except for a little difficulty in cutting the symbolic ribbon, the shindig came off as smoothly as jet planes from a carrier deck.

V-Day in Double Measure

V-Day was Viaduct Day and Victory Day; a triumph in double measure!

Years of planning and watching and waiting suddenly bloomed like a ten-bloom Easter lily.

The Seattle Sunday Times, April 5, 1953, page 1.

stood a lovely coastal range, the Olympic Mountains. Day trips to the rivers, valleys and slopes of these marvels of nature were an easy drive or ferryboat ride.

"Mediocre" best described the Seattle Symphony. There was the University of Washington, a respectable regional school; the Boeing Company, famous for building B-17 bombers that helped win World War II, a good but boutique (Asian) art museum; and the minor-league Seattle Rainiers. UW sports teams, however, grabbed most of the headlines. One provincial marker of the city was its "purple and gold" character, the colors of the UW, whose graduates tended to populate if not dominate many local institutions and businesses.

Yet Seattle could boast no more than two or three restaurants of high quality, the kind to write home about. Live theater was limited: the Showboat and the Aqua Theatre at Green Lake, where "The

Aqua Follies of 1953" was on the bill. In addition to a smattering of neighborhood movie houses, there were five major movie palaces, built in the grand style of the 1920s. At one, the spacious but aging Orpheum on the corner of Fifth Avenue and Stewart Street, Warner Bros.' *The Charge at Feather River* was playing in 3-D, with Guy Madison and Frank Lovejoy in the lead roles. The Alaskan Way Viaduct, screening off the city's downtown waterfront, opened for traffic. Voters approved expanding the city north to Northeast 145th Street. Unions struck *The Seattle Times*.

Each summer, the first weekend in August, the Seafair festival drew large crowds to its many events: kids' parades in neighborhood business districts, a beauty pageant to select Miss Seafair and the rowdy but harmless Seafair Pirates. Seafair's twin crown jewels were the Torchlight Parade and, the grand finale, the Gold Cup hydroplane races where local auto dealer Stan Sayres' *Slo-mo-shun* racing boats dominated the competition. To watch the race, up to 100,000 people (sporting generous stocks of libations) lined the shores of Lake Washington or occupied their boats along the infamous log boom that formed the eastern boundary of the three-mile oval race course.

Seattle's population of about 470,000 included an African-American community largely confined to the city's east-central area south of Madison Street, and an Asian population mostly Filipino, Chinese and Japanese, in the area along Jackson Street, Rainier Valley and Beacon Hill. The city was not integrated. Housing was not open. In social terms, Seattle was "white bread," steady and solid, a good place to raise a family — especially if you were white.

Downtown, the stately Rainier Club serviced the wealthy but allowed no women members, certainly no minorities. Strict state "blue laws" permitted no liquor sales on Sundays. Nor could any alcoholic beverages be sold within a quarter-mile of the UW campus — which, of course, did not prevent well-stocked cabinets in fraternities and sororities from containing the ingredients for refreshments of an alcoholic content. Gambling was against the law. Yet financial stakes at Rainier Club bridge tables, or in poker games in such gathering spots as the Roman Catholic Knights of Columbus or labor union halls, were well known and tolerated, some even partaken in by Seattle's elected and appointed officials. Mahjong parlors and clandestine spots for furtive dice games could be found with little effort.

The "Queen City," as some called it then, maintained a very different form of tolerance than would prevail some three decades later.

Political power in Seattle resided primarily with mainstream conservative Republicans. There existed a de facto interlocking directorate that ran things, controlling Seattle City Hall and the King County Courthouse. The political axis allied the Central Association, essentially the downtown real estate owners and investors, and the Chamber of Commerce, each redolent of middle-American Babbittry, dominated by banks, law firms, big medical institutions and several prominent businesses and established families. The Municipal League of Seattle acted as a good-government organization, and tilted Republican. It was dominated by business-oriented citizens and financed largely by business memberships.

In the "control room" for this power structure sat Charles O. Carroll, the Republican King County Prosecutor, and Mort Frayn, chairman of the King County Republican Party. This potent duo called many if not most of the shots: who might run for office, who would get establishment financing and other means of support, and what would take priority on the public agenda.

The League of Women Voters, though more progressive, represented mainline views well within the established good-government frame of reference.

Thus, Seattle-King County stood as a kind of Republican redoubt amid a state with some important Democratic leanings. At the state level power was shared. Democrats held the two U.S. Senate seats (Warren G. Magnuson and Henry "Scoop" Jackson). The state's U.S. House of Representatives delegation was controlled by Republicans, as was the governor's chair, filled by Arthur B. Langlie (until 1956, when Democrat Albert Rosellini succeeded him). Seattle's two daily news papers, the Hearst-owned morning *Post-Intelligencer* and the local Blethen family's evening *The Times*, could be counted on as reliable supporters for this political arrangement, each predictably Republican.

Local opposition in Seattle consisted primarily of holdover components of the old New Deal coalition assembled by the late President Franklin D. Roosevelt: labor unions, intellectuals and professionals, and blue-collar workers. Labor town Seattle's strong unions included the powerful longshoremen, the teamsters, the machinists, transit drivers and electrical workers. There were prominent Democrats among the faculty at the University of Washington and in some of the law firms. And there were the King County Democratic Party's district organizations. Counted among these but not formally organized — yet — stood the "Stevenson Democrats," or progressives. Liberal, smart and well-connected, this assemblage included Kay and Stim Bullitt.

These loosely organized liberals congealed during the '50s into an active corps of advocates for change. They discussed a range of issues. Primary in their sights were peace and avoidance of another world war (now that America possessed the atomic bomb), civil rights with an emphasis on the rights of black citizens in Southern states, resistance to the "witch-hunts" of right-wingers into so-called "un-American" activities of their political enemies, even such topics as "are U.S. corporations too big?" They were known as the Keechelus group. They held annual weekend conferences at the Keechelus Inn (later demolished to make way for construction of Interstate 90 through Snoqualmie Pass) at Lake Keechelus. They held other meetings and conferences, including some at a former Civilian Conservation Corps camp (now Camp Waskowitz) in North Bend, some in town. Largely, but not exclusively comprising lawyers and law students, the Keechelus group included people like Stim, and later Kay, John Goldmark, King County Commissioner Ed Munro (and his young son Allan), Bob Block, Walter Walkinshaw, James Wilson, John F. Robinson, Solie Ringold, David Sprague, Ken MacDonald, Donald Schmechel, Brock Adams and Fred Bassetti. In 1956, they would formally incorporate themselves as the Metropolitan Democratic Club (MDC), and would include U.S. Senators Magnuson and Jackson.

These liberals and moderates, however earnest, talented and full of promise, had yet to have their innings. They remained on the periphery of the action. In the mid-1950s, they were part of the seeds of change germinating just below the surface of staid, provincial Seattle. By the end of the decade, however, they would be among the agents of change who would help reinvent this Northwest seaport town into a vibrant urban metropolis.

Boeing's Dash 80, prototype for what would be the immensely successful 707 airliner.

Harbingers

At its manufacturing plant in Renton, The Boeing Company rolled out its "Dash-80," prototype for the 707 that would be the game-changing four-engine passenger jet that would launch the age of popular air travel and shrink the world. In place were Washington state's two United States senators, "Maggie" and "Scoop," Democrats who over time would rise to great influence and power and bring home a rich menu of benefits that would help to elevate and expand the city's cultural offerings, including money to establish a civic cultural center that would become home to Seattle's successful 1962 World's Fair. Plans were made to overhaul local government that would lead to the creation of Metro, the Municipality of Metropolitan Seattle. Those progressive Democrats were hard at work pushing for open-housing laws, fairness in employment practices, as well as assaults on other racial barriers built in and around Seattle. These were but some of the seedlings that signaled the coming changes. Even with the failed attempts to establish racial integration, those efforts nevertheless schooled a community that would make social progress in the decade to come.

No abbreviated discussion of 1950s Seattle, King County and the state of Washington should ignore the vicious and hurtful attacks mounted by right-wing Republicans against alleged communists. It poisoned the atmosphere, even for the nonpolitical. This was the heyday of McCarthyite witchhunts that became obsessive spectacles in the guilt-by-association fashion of U.S. Sen. Joseph McCarthy, Republican from Wisconsin. In Seattle Dr. Melvin Rader, a UW philosophy professor, and Margaret Ceis were among the targets of these Gestapo-like tactics to ferret out and persecute people with liberal sympathies, particularly those who had affiliated with Communist groups in the 1930s but long since renounced them.

Fortunately, this "gang" was discredited by none other than *The Seattle Times*. Investigative reporter Ed Guthman delved deeply into the Rader case. He wrote a series of articles that completely exonerated the professor. In the bargain, Guthman's work won the newspaper's first Pulitzer Prize for investigative reporting. Guthman would go on to become a member of U.S. Sen. Robert Kennedy's staff.

Many liberals, like Kay Bullitt, favored some socialist-like policies and programs: peace initiatives, national health insurance, public housing for the low-income. Kay, for instance, like the majority of liberals, opposed totalitarianism, strongly favored democracy and conducted her public activities well within the letter and spirit of traditional American political principles and practices. Yet, even as McCarthyism faded from the scene, organizations such as the John Birch Society, including an active chapter in Washington's Republican Party, continued the scurrilous accusatory practices branding people as Communist.

This labeling as "communist" was applied by some to people and institutions that were liberal and community focused. For example, Group Health Cooperative, founded in 1947 and "dedicated to making quality health care available and affordable," suffered such slings and arrows from within the medical community and the larger community where the kinder skeptics regarded it as "socialist." Group Health was a nonprofit. Many thought the fledgling co-op could not survive the larger, long-standing medical institutions that operated on a for-profit model.

These mean-spirited people, in proof of the law of unintended consequences, contributed to the liberalizing of Seattle and King County politics. In that endeavor, Kay Bullitt and company would help lead the way.

Kay, William, Margaret, Barney and Marion.

Chapter 2

Serious people, strong personalities

> Marion wanted her girls to
> grow up as she had, prepared
> for "an interesting life."

Kay Squire Muller

On February 22, 1925, Katharine Squire Muller became the second daughter of Marion Churchill Muller and William Augustus Muller. Like her older sister, Marion (Barney), and yet-to-come Margaret, she was born in Boston and grew up at the family home in Arlington, a suburban town just to the northwest of Cambridge. Their early years would anticipate the full flowering of the women's movement that blossomed in the 1960s. Their mother was a professional in her own right, and also wanted her girls to grow up as she had, prepared for "an interesting life."

By the time Marion married William Muller, she already had established herself as both an educator and a leader. She graduated from Radcliffe College in 1906; taught school in Newton and Brookline, Massachusetts; and served as dean of women at the prestigious Colorado College, out west in the Rocky Mountains. Marion was 38 when she married William, a man 18 years her senior. Muller had graduated from Harvard in 1891 and attended classes with W.E.B. Du Bois, a prominent leader for African-American rights and founder of the National Association for the Advancement of Colored People. Muller, a businessman, worked primarily in insurance and real estate. A moderate New England Republican, he was actively involved in the Congregational Church. The Muller family attended the Old South Church in Boston — where Samuel Adams launched the famous original Tea Party of the American Revolution. Sadly, William died when Kay was 16, leaving Marion to raise their three girls alone.

The example and tone Marion set for her daughters was one of leadership and activism. "Mother served on the board of the Window Shop, a store and restaurant that provided employment for Jewish refugees," Kay recalls. "But first of all she was a teacher. She ran the Women's Educational and Industrial Union in Boston." Life in Arlington was good. Although Kay remembers admiring a lovely home next door, built during the Revolutionary War period, that was demolished and "replaced by a gas station!"

Kay attended the private Shady Hill School through the ninth grade, and says "I loved ninth grade because we got to perform Gilbert and Sullivan's *Princess Ida* operetta." She also studied piano with Mrs. Doering. She learned to play classical music and developed a preference for Mozart.

For high school, she was enrolled at Concord Academy. Much of what Kay is known and respected for today began to blossom

Shady Hill School

At Shady Hill, students are taught to think, to question, and to consider multiple perspectives before transforming their ideas into meaningful action. This tradition of learning has served our students well for over 95 years, since the school was founded on the back porch of the Hocking family home in Cambridge.

— From the Shady Hill School website

during these formative teenage years. She had become a fan of Paul Robeson. He was a student on an academic scholarship at Rutgers, where he earned All-American honors as a football player and served as his class's valedictorian. He earned a law degree from Columbia Law School in 1922, while playing professional football, yet he was not allowed to practice law, Kay remembers, because he was black. He became a highly acclaimed actor and singer who openly promoted civil rights, spoke out against fascism and opposed imperialism. His recording of "Ballad for Americans" caught Kay's attention. She heard him sing in concert, both in Cambridge and in New York City. Two stanzas from the ballad are:

A man in white skin can never be free while his black brother
     is in slavery,
And we here highly resolve that these dead shall not have died
     in vain.
And this government of the people, by the people and for the
     people
Shall not perish from the Earth.
Abraham Lincoln said that on November 19, 1863, at
     Gettysburg, Pennsylvania.
And he was right. I believe that too.

Say, we still don't know who you are, mister.
Well, I started to tell you ...
The machine age came with a great big roar,
As America grew in peace and war.
And a million wheels went around and 'round.
The cities reached into the sky,
And dug down deep into the ground.
And some got rich and some got poor.
But the people carried through,
So our country grew.

Kay's interest in history and government led her to read about the World War I battle of Verdun, in which close to a million soldiers on both sides lost their lives or suffered wounds. The account revealed that the crosses marking the graves of Allied soldiers were white. But those for the "enemy" were black. She pondered this and thought that all the dead were part of the human family. This reflection inspired her to write a poem in which she describes a snowfall that covers all the crosses in white. Her poem was published in the Concord Academy magazine. At age 14, Kay had become an activist.

Graduating from Concord in 1942, just as the United States became involved in World War II, Kay, like her mother, went to Radcliffe College. Men were off to war, and she remembers that "women students received the full attention of the Harvard professors." Kay studied government, fully expecting she would go to work in Washington, D.C. But her college years were not limited to studies alone. She grew in substance and scope, absorbing new experiences and probing wider horizons.

As a freshman, Kay was invited to a special dinner honoring first lady Eleanor Roosevelt. Radcliffe was inducting Mrs. Roosevelt into the school's Phi Beta Kappa chapter as an honorary member. Roosevelt's remarks made a lasting imprint on Kay, who remembers her admonishing the students: "Never mistake knowledge for wisdom: One helps you make a living; the other helps you make a life."

Outside school, Kay tutored young students in biology and Latin in Somerville and Pocasset, Massachusetts. Importantly, she was one of 10 young women who spent the summer of 1944 at the Hampton Institute, an interracial farm camp in Virginia. Five white and five black young women comprised the program that involved doing farm chores. "We made a trip over to Colonial Williamsburg. I saw my first 'whites only' sign posted above a drinking fountain. It was awful," she frowns. "We only could eat in restaurants that served black people. We swam in a blacks-only swimming pool and slept in a dormitory at a school for black students because the black women in our group weren't allowed in whites-only hotels."

Kay's activism only accelerated. The Massachusetts Legislature took up a bill to establish a Fair Employment Practices Commission. Fresh from her Hampton Institute summer, Kay went to a legislative hearing on the bill and testified in its favor. A few weeks later, she was in the visitors' gallery when the FEPC bill came up for a vote and was walking out when one of the legislators approached her. He complimented Kay on her earlier testimony and offered to give her a ride back to school. Kay accepted. On the drive back, the legislator wanted to hear more about Kay's summer at the Hampton Institute. Kay obliged. Her legislator-driver was Thomas P. ("Tip") O'Neill.

Some days later, Radcliffe's president summoned Kay to his office. An unnamed person had complained to him about the testimony of a Radcliffe student in support of the Fair Employment Practices Commission that the complainant believed to reflect poorly on the college. Kay acknowledged she had so testified. For his part, the president complimented her for her effort, and Kay left in the knowledge she enjoyed the backing of Radcliffe's top leader. As for O'Neill, he was elected speaker of the Massachusetts House of Representatives in 1949. Three years later, in 1952, he won Boston's 11th Congressional District seat vacated by U.S. Rep. John F. Kennedy, who had won election to the U.S. Senate. That same year, "Scoop" Jackson won his seat in the Senate from our state. Jackson and Kennedy would become friends and political allies. In 1977, O'Neill was chosen as speaker of the U.S. House of Representatives.

Kay challenged another barrier in 1945. She and a group of young Radcliffe women mounted a challenge to the Harvard rowing team. Crew racing was the exclusive domain of men in those days. "They weren't Harvard's top rowers, with the war on and all," Kay recalls. "But they were game." The Radcliffe challengers did not even have a racing shell, so they borrowed one from a local boys' high school. It was a short race on the Charles River, between two bridges.

As the race was about to start, from under the bridge there appeared a crew from MIT (Massachusetts Institute of Technology), all dressed as women. "We weren't very good," Kay says. "But the judges declared us the winner because they ruled the Harvard crew did not cross the finish line."

Radcliffe's victory produced some lasting resentment. So upset was the Harvard Alumni Association, Kay recalls, that they turned to the Harvard president, who arranged "to prevent women from

They beat Harvard! From left: Jane and Dolly Driscoll, Phyllis Cronin, Pata Lewis, Eleanor Merrick, Kay Muller, Lynn Baker, Louise Florencourt.

rowing on the Charles River until 1972." At the same time, when Radcliffe rowers asked their school president to buy them a racing shell, he refused. The 1972 enactment of Title IX into federal law eliminated this sexist silliness. Today Radcliffe's rowing program rates among the top in the East.

In the spring of 1946, Kay graduated from Radcliffe magna cum laude and was inducted into the national honors society Phi Beta Kappa. She held a Bachelor of Arts degree in government. Now her career could begin in full.

For her senior thesis, Kay had written about the role of the federal government in education. But instead of looking for work in Washington, D.C., as she had thought she would, she decided to learn more about education by going back to Shady Hill. There, she became an apprentice teacher in the fourth grade. As luck would have it, the fourth grade teacher she supported went on a maternity leave of absence. Kay was promoted to take her place. She taught fourth grade at Shady Hill for five "wonderful" years. "I really loved that age group," she says affectionately.

Shady Hill provided Kay Muller with more than a teaching experience. In the summers of 1949 and 1950, Kay spent time with a group of American educators, including Shady Hill's headmistress Katharine Taylor, helping their German counterparts to learn of advances made in early childhood education in the United States during World War II. To help pay for her trip, she quit smoking, setting aside the money she would have spent buying cigarettes. It was a "two-fer": save money, improve her health.

Postwar Europe was struggling to recover from six years of horrible carnage and devastation. Germany was divided into four zones: the east controlled by the Soviet Union, with the United States, France and Great Britain each controlling a zone in what became West Germany. Berlin, surrounded by and located inside the eastern zone, was divided in two, with the Soviets controlling the eastern portion, the Allies the western. The Cold War was in full swing.

In 1948, the Soviets sealed off the Western allies' half of Berlin, an act of aggression that drew a stout response. The United States, under President Harry Truman, with support from Great Britain and France, organized a massive airlift to supply food and other necessities to the beleaguered city. The airlift lasted more than a year before the Soviets backed down. Yet, the summertime education program in which Kay participated forged ahead under the auspices of the Unitarian Service Committee and Child Care Institute in Germany.

That first summer, in 1949, Kay's group worked in Vöhl, near Marburg Castle in central West Germany, and the following year in both Berlin and Hanover. "I saw people living in bombed-out buildings and open spaces — you could see right in," Kay remembers. She witnessed other circumstances revealing the plight and desperation of the German people: "We had gone into East Berlin to see a play that was in German. We stepped outside during the intermission and someone in our party tossed a cigarette butt over to the curb. Suddenly, a crowd rushed over to pick it up. It was sad. People worried we might be detained by the East German or Soviet authorities that day. But we made it back OK."

Witnessing firsthand the heaps of rubble from the Allies' incessant bombing of Berlin, the city's hollowed-out buildings where only portions of skeletal walls stood in silent testimony to the pervasive devastation, and the survivors searching for scraps of food, sticks of wood for a fire's warmth, even discarded cigarette butts: These tableaus imprinted indelibly on Kay Muller's mind and reinforced her pacifist convictions and her determination to work for peace.

Among the friendships made during her work in Germany was Hildegard Hamm-Brücher, a chemist and member of the liberal Free Democratic Party. Hamm-Brücher held a seat on the Munich City Council, and one day she would stand unsuccessfully as her party's candidate for the presidency of the Federal Republic of Germany. She made a strong impression on Kay. They formed a lasting friendship and Hamm-Brücher would become godmother to Kay's firstborn, Dorothy.

Back at Shady Hill, teaching allowed Kay to remain engaged in politics. She volunteered some of her spare time working as the unpaid secretary to Harvard historian Arthur M. Schlesinger Jr., in his capacity as president of the Cambridge chapter of Americans for Democratic Action (ADA). Schlesinger was among the founding members of the ADA. This work allowed Kay to meet the prominent Harvard economist John Kenneth Galbraith. But Kay's itch to move beyond the precincts of Boston-Cambridge-Arlington began to intensify. She elected to take a year off and travel, but for a purpose.

"I had noticed that the kids in our school in Cambridge were not involved in their communities," Kay recalls. "I wanted to find out if other cities involved their youths in their communities."

One reason she came to Seattle was to see a friend who was away climbing mountains in Alaska. But his return to Seattle was "delayed." Kay's plan was to stay about two weeks but she stayed two months.

It was summer 1951. She found a room in a house just north of the University of Washington, met some "very nice people" and got to know the city. By November she was off to Oregon and California to visit her sister Margaret in San Francisco. Kay discovered that "Margie" was experiencing some mental health problems. The two drove to Los Angeles, where Margaret could stay with their older sister, Barney, while Kay went on to Mexico to attend a conference of the Second International Congress on Mental Health.

On the last day of the conference, Kay met a psychiatrist from Nicaragua. As they discussed the status of mental health care in his country, he told her that a person seeking mental health treatment could only make one hospital visit per month to one of only two mental health hospitals there. The conference ended and Kay returned to Los Angeles.

Her sister required some medical attention. So Kay and Margie packed up their belongings and headed east, by car, to return home. "So I didn't really do what I set out to do," Kay notes. Margaret needed help. Kay provided it.

It was spring 1952. The U.S. presidential campaign was warming up. Retired World War II hero Gen. Dwight D. Eisenhower, president of Columbia University, was considered the favorite to win the Republican nomination. As it turned out, Illinois Gov. Adlai Stevenson won the Democratic nod. Kay signed up to support him and returned to teach at Shady Hill that fall, this time teaching second grade.

American voters chose Gen. Eisenhower to be their president, ending 20 years of White House dominance by the Democrats. Paralleling that political transition was one Kay Muller undertook herself. As the school year came to an end in the spring of 1953, this young woman who had seen war-ravaged Europe and become a pacifist, who had experienced racism up close and personal and spoken up for equality for black American citizens, who thought there could be better methods and approaches to educating children, who had gained some knowledge and contact with mental health issues, was ready for a change. She moved to Seattle.

Charles Stimson Bullitt

That Kay Muller would be attracted to "Stim" Bullitt contains no mystery.

Well educated, well informed politically and very well con-nected, Charles Stimson "Stim" Bullitt presented a man active in life and committed to many of the same causes as Kay. He was born in

1919 to Dorothy Stimson and Alexander Scott Bullitt, a prominent Seattle couple, each in her and his own right.

Dorothy was born on Queen Anne Hill, educated in the East and focused on civic matters and the arts. Her father, Charles Douglas Stimson, known as C.D., made a huge success of the lumber business and invested heavily in Seattle real estate, where he financed the Olympic Hotel, the Stimson Building and the Coliseum Theatre among other buildings. Her mother was among the founders of Children's Hospital, the Seattle Symphony and the Visiting Nurse Service.

Scott Bullitt had met his wife, Dorothy, at a childhood friend's wedding (his brother was the groom), and after a brief stay in Louisville, the Bullitts settled in Seattle, where Scott joined his father-in-law in the commercial real estate business. Bullitt brought his degree from Princeton University and a deep involvement in southern Democratic politics to a community dominated by northern Republicans. According to HistoryLink.org, "He organized the Democratic Party in Washington State. He mentored U.S. Senator Warren G. Magnuson in the early years of his political career, but was unsuccessful in his own bids for senator and governor."

Bullitt was a Seattle Municipal League member who reached across party lines but, sadly, died of colon cancer in 1932, shortly before he was to nominate New York Gov. Franklin D. Roosevelt for president at that year's Democratic convention. At age 40, having no business experience, his widow, whose father and brother also had recently died, was left alone to run one of the West's largest commercial real estate businesses while raising three children: Stim, age 12; Priscilla ("Patsy") 11; and Harriet, 8. She proved to be more than up to the task.

In 1947 she purchased the license of a small, not very successful radio station. Believing in the future of television and FM radio, she would build from that small beginning the highly successful and widely respected King Broadcasting Company, which grew over the next 30 years to include stations and cable broadcast systems throughout the Northwest and Hawaii.

The awarding of a license for Seattle's first television station demonstrated Dorothy Bullitt's prowess as a businesswoman. When her King Broadcasting Company renamed the little newly acquired station KING TV, Seattle had not many more than 6,000 television sets. Even so, the station was an instant hit and sales of TV sets around the area soared. KING TV's Channel 5 affiliated

Dorothy S. Bullitt and King Broadcasting Co.

In her application to the Federal Communications Commission, she promised to provide at least 100 minutes per week of public service

Dorothy S. Bullitt in her office at King Broadcasting.

announcements. She and her talented administrative team gave staff the support and editorial license to deal with controversial topics. She had a firm policy against selling air time to religious organizations, but donated such time, most notably to her own St. Mark's Episcopal Cathedral, for the Christmas Eve midnight service and for the weekly Sunday-evening compline service.

— HistoryLink.org

with the American Broadcasting Company (ABC), a much weaker broadcasting network than either the National Broadcasting Company (NBC) or the Columbia Broadcasting System (CBS). In the local scramble to get into the television business, the staunchly Republican Fisher family, owners of Fisher Flouring Mills and the long-established KOMO AM Radio, won the NBC network affiliation from the head of RCA Victor, Gen. David Sarnoff, who owned NBC. The Fishers put their Channel 4 television station on the air in 1952. But Mrs. Bullitt's station was a popular success. Still, it was a shock of no small magnitude when Mrs. Bullitt returned from a quiet visit to New York and Gen. Sarnoff with the NBC affiliation. KOMO was forced to affiliate with ABC.

Dorothy S. Bullitt's success was remarkable. At a time when women were expected to be either at home or involved in civic and charity works (noblesse oblige), far removed from the man's world of commerce and finance, she was a recognized business leader. Mrs. Bullitt also was a prominent Democrat, well acquainted with President Franklin Delano Roosevelt (FDR), his New Deal Administration, as well as up-and-coming state Democrats Warren Magnuson and U.S. Sen. Hugh Mitchell. With young Stim in tow, she had attended the 1932 Democratic National Convention, where her late husband had been slated to deliver the speech nominating FDR. Her son, who had idolized his father, soaked up these activities and political points of view, leaving an indelible political imprint upon him that he would develop and polish and live by as the years unfolded.

Stim's sister Harriet, commenting years later on her brother's idealized view of his father, said, "He thought our father was perfect, and he wasn't perfect."

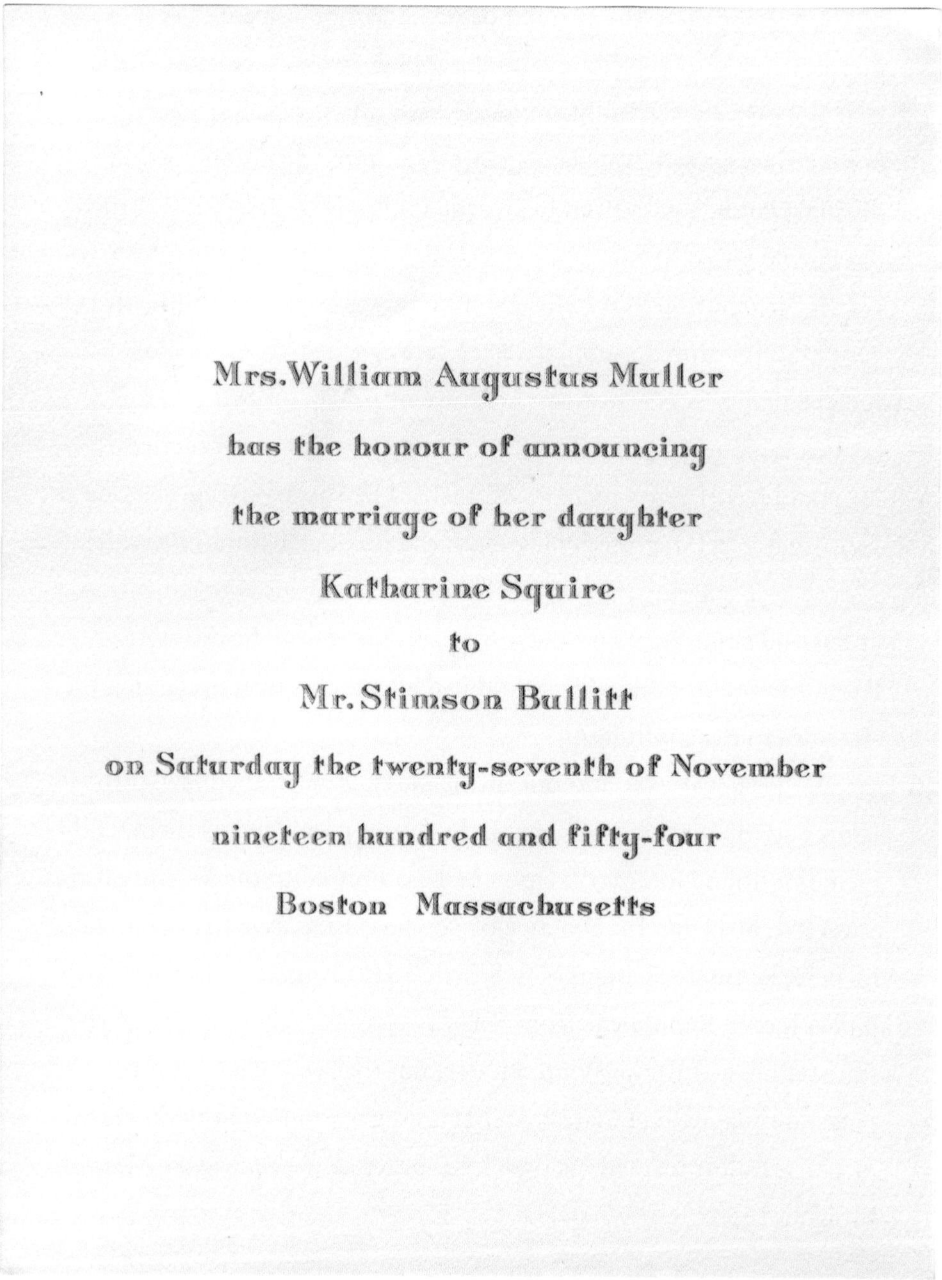

Mrs. William Augustus Muller

has the honour of announcing

the marriage of her daughter

Katharine Squire

to

Mr. Stimson Bullitt

on Saturday the twenty-seventh of November

nineteen hundred and fifty-four

Boston   Massachusetts

Stim grew up in the Highlands neighborhood, a gated community northwest of the city overlooking Puget Sound. During World War II, Navy Lt. j.g. Bullitt requested sea duty — he had been a boxing champion at Yale University — suffered a shrapnel wound during a landing assault in Leyte, the Philippines, and was awarded the Purple Heart.

By virtue of birth into his prominent, wealthy and politically active family, Stim developed a keen sense of justice, espousing racial equality, social justice, the cause of peace, protections for his beloved environment and responsibility in business practices. He could have been a yachtsman. Instead he chose boxing, the one sport that was integrated. He even faced boxing champion Archie Moore as a sparring partner. Despite the fact of his elite education at Lakeside and Yale, and the resources to live well, he did not flaunt the Bullitt name. He would live his life this way, preferring the shadows to the spotlights.

With the war over and out of the Navy, Stim studied law at the University of Washington. He made several good friends there, including John Goldmark. Upon being admitted to the Washington State Bar, he began the practice of law but also was active politically. In 1952, he ran for Congress in Seattle's 1st Congressional District. Bullitt lost to Republican Tom Pelly, as Gen. Eisenhower carried the state on his way to the White House. But that year Democrat Henry Jackson took a U.S. Senate seat, beginning a tenure that would last 31 years. Bullitt formed his own legal practice with partners Marvin Mohl and Jonathan Whetzel.

Meanwhile, his first marriage, to Spokane-born, Sarah Lawrence-educated Carolyn Kizer, added trouble on a personal level. Kizer had threatened to appear at some of Stim's political campaign appearances and to openly criticize him, remembers his friend and fellow Democrat Allan Munro: "This hurt him a lot." Soon, Stim's marriage to Kizer — a celebrated poet with a prickly personality who would win the Pulitzer Prize in 1985 and the Theodore Roethke Memorial Poetry Prize in 1988 — ended in divorce. Friends remember this marriage as an unhappy one, despite the arrival of three children. The open, increasingly hostile relations between Carolyn and Stim adversely affected their children — collateral damage that would impact their lives for years to come. The family had been living on rural Squak Mountain near undeveloped Issaquah, an out-of-the-city, little-social-life location that Kizer despised.

Bullitt had bought a large in-city lot on Capitol Hill, planning to build a house there. The property at 1125 Harvard Avenue East sat amid many fine large, classic homes built in the early 20th century. Bullitt initially retained the pre-eminent Seattle modernist architect Paul Thiry to design his house. Due to the divorce, it was never built. Instead, upon his marriage to Kay, Stim hired young Fred Bassetti to create a different structure at 1125 for his new wife and his three children, whose custody he shared with Kizer.

Stim's second run for Congress, in 1954, resulted in another defeat in the primary to former U.S. Sen. Hugh Mitchell, who in turn lost to incumbent Republican Tom Pelly.

The loss ended Stim's career in electoral politics but his interest and involvement in public affairs remained as strong as ever. Racial equality became a prime cause. Already, according to HistoryLink.org,

> He had in 1941 recommended an African American friend with a master's degree from Yale for an elementary school teaching position with the Seattle School District. Seattle

School Superintendent Worth McClure wrote in reply that
the Seattle school system did not hire Negroes.

Bullitt was on the Committee for a Washington Law
Against Discrimination, a sponsor of the Washington State
Fair Employment Practice Committee, sat on the board of the
Seattle Urban League, and was later a trustee of the American
Civil Liberties Union of Washington.

Stim Bullitt was a student of all he did, probing, learning
and reflecting on his experiences. He set about putting down his
thoughts and observations about politics and particularly the experiences and demands placed on people who run for office. The result
was a highly praised book, *To Be a Politician*, published in 1959. It
won favorable reviews in, among others, *The New Yorker*, *The New
York Times* and the *New York Review of Books*. Sociologist and
attorney David Riesman wrote a laudatory forward for the book. Its
publication marked Bullitt as a serious and thoughtful commenta-
tor, capable of work at a high level on the national stage. It would
not be his last substantial contribution to earn major attention.
Published by Doubleday & Company, the first edition contained
a dedication "To Kay." She had done the painstaking work of
copyediting his manuscript. Second and third editions contained no
such — or any other — dedication.

If Stim Bullitt was a good attorney, a deep thinker, an accomplished rock climber and mountaineer, a distinguished war veteran,
a caring father — and he was *all* those things — he also was a
"painfully shy man." Family and friends alike describe him as at
times possessed of a powerful sense of inadequacy. He could be at
ease among only a few very close colleagues. Typically, he eschewed
the limelight and often would stand off to himself in gatherings,
even at home. Perhaps this helps to explain his love of the outdoors,

devotion to climbing — especially some of the toughest peaks — and the peace and tranquillity he could find in the bosom of nature. He enjoyed the challenge of taking on rugged climbs, often leading the way up well ahead of younger climbers. In town, the lush, open space in the yard at 1125 provided him an urban respite of a kind.

1125 Harvard Avenue East shortly after completion.

Chapter 3

1125 Harvard East

"Fred Bassetti told my dad that
Stim wanted him to design this
'gawd-damned ski lodge'
— an A-frame house built at 1125."

— Kenan Block, son of
Bob and Dorothy Block

An A-frame, poorly planned and executed in this upscale, well-maintained turn-of-the-20th-century neighborhood of mansions — and recently built but classically designed townhomes — might have become the neighborhood's ugly duckling. Not so. The "ski lodge" is a warm, welcoming, if unusual structure that sits back off the street, in the northeast quadrant of the expansive 1 3/4-acre lot. A large laurel hedge, thick shrubs and tall trees screen the building from Harvard Avenue East.

The full exterior is best seen from inside the yard. It is an A-frame, no doubt. Yet it offers grace and appeal that invites a visitor to want more, to be inside, where likely thousands in total have been since Kay and Stim moved in that Christmas Eve, 1955. They had married on November 27, 1954.

Kay remembers thinking, "It was kind of mean the house was built so close to Mr. Bloedel. But he never said anything about it to us. I do love it so much. I had never seen an A-frame. He [Bassetti] built a model for us. I didn't spend too much time worrying what the neighbors would think."

The home's footprint is a basic rectangle, on a north-south axis, congruent with the north-south shape of this large rectangular property. Attached on the east is a slim, rectangular structure that contains the private quarters. One enters the house from the north side, having walked in from Harvard past a driveway, then turning south toward the front door. The light and wood-dominated interior makes an immediate warm and welcoming impression.

On the west side of the building is the living room, open and spacious all the way to the peak of the A.

Large windows provide light and a view of the grounds to the west, down a slope to the trees and houses beyond on Boylston Avenue East. Among its most prominent features are the warmth and openness provided by generous uses of wood and windows.

› Large triangular windows form the top portion of the north wall and rest on granite; *Entropy*, a modern art piece by her grandson Ben Schmechel, hangs just to the left of the fireplace hood and chimney.

› The metal, freestanding fireplace sits on a granite ledge that stretches the length of the north wall about 18 inches up from the terrazzo floor.

Entropy by grandson Ben Schmechel won "best in show" in an art competition for Seattle eighth graders.

› Windows form the west wall and offer views of the yard and through the trees and shrubs some glimpses of Queen Anne Hill, Gas Works Park and the north end of Lake Union.

› A sliding glass door opens onto a sizable patio where a round table, with a center hole for a sun umbrella, is large enough to seat eight people. In the direction of the yard, a Gerard Tsutakawa fountain provides a soothing trickle of flowing water that fills the space with a refreshing sense of peace and contentment.

› South of the living room, the kitchen contains a small space with a table where Kay takes meals, or a break and a cup of tea. The kitchen's prime feature is the window (added in a later remodel) affording a survey of the yard that may be a dog run, host to any number of games from badminton to soccer, Greek plays, weddings and memorials. A swing hangs from the massive English elm tree (officially designated as Seattle's first Heritage Tree). Kay's famous summer picnics are held here. Says she: "I love my kitchen, looking out the window. I like cooking breakfast. But I am not excited about cooking generally."

› The upper level or balcony overlooks the spacious living room below and provides a second-story lookout south and west to the yard. A couch faces west in front of a round coffee table and chairs resting on oak floors, another gathering spot for a small group. Windows form the west wall and add light and more views out toward Queen Anne Hill. Kay does most of her writing (by hand) here, using pen and lined yellow pads.

› The stairway to and from the balcony leads to a narrow hallway past the front door to the east side of the house, to its more private spaces: bedrooms, a den and small office, and of course bathrooms.

› Two bedrooms were added on at the south side when Kay was expecting her second child.

› A basement allows for storage and a workshop for arts and crafts. It has a small stage where the kids put on informal plays and played games.

1125 had been part of Seattle's history long before Stim Bullitt bought it. Some of the homes in the area had been planned with the help of the internationally prominent Olmsted (step) brothers (Frederick Law Olmsted Jr. and John Charles Olmsted), leading landscape architects of their day.

According to an unsigned one-page history of "The Bullitt Residence" in Kay's files,

The property was originally owned by the Horace Henry family. The house was in the center of the lot. The barn at the north end housed the first art gallery in Seattle. Mr. Henry provided the gallery at the University of Washington for the art.

Rooms built in the wall on Prospect Street housed horses, tack and a sleigh brought from Minnesota. The stairs leading to the abandoned Boylston St. on the west were part of the original Olmsted design for the garden.

The Henry family moved to the Highlands, and after Mr. Henry died his sons gave the house and land to the City of Seattle for a library to be named for [their mother] Susan Henry. The city decided to build the library further south near the commercial area and took down the house. The property was sold to Mr. [Prentice] Bloedel, who lived next door.

Prior to their move to the Highlands in 1940, the Henrys donated their admired art collection to the University of Washington, where it now is seen at the respected Henry Art Gallery, which they financed. Bloedel, founder of MacMillan Bloedel Ltd., a second-generation Northwest lumberman, sold the property to Stim "at a very reasonable price" according to Kay, but with a condition: that only one house be built on the site (it was zoned for up to 13 houses) until Mr. Bloedel died. Relishing the property's open space, Stim readily agreed.

The Henry Siegl Quintet warms up to perform, clockwise from left: Henry Siegl, William Bailey, James Harnett, Don Bushell and Norma Durst.

Photo courtesy of the *P-I* Collection, MOHAI.

Chapter 4

Setting up house

Among the first performances
at 1125 was a concert by the
Henry Siegl Quartet led by the Seattle
Symphony's concert master.

Connecting

Once in Seattle, Kay wasted no time getting involved. She found
a job as an educational counselor at a psychiatric clinic in the
University District. She joined the League of Women Voters, as
well as the local chapters of the American Civil Liberties Union
and Americans for Democratic Action. In light of their civic and
political interests (Stim being president of the local ADA,) it seems
almost inevitable that Kay and Stim would cross paths.

Enter the Block family. Dorothy Block, wife of Seattle investment banker Robert J. "Bob" Block, had met Kay's sister Barney
while taking a course from cultural anthropologist Margaret Mead

at Wellesley College. Kay was invited to a dinner party hosted by Phyllis Lamphere at the Washington Athletic Club to honor the visiting president of Lamphere's alma mater, Barnard College. Years later, Lamphere would be elected to the Seattle City Council, followed by service as regional director for the U.S. Department of Commerce's Economic Development Administration under President Jimmy Carter. During the evening Kay met Bob and Dorothy Block. Quickly, they became friends.

Dorothy Block shared Kay's interest in education, political points of view and civic activism. Soon, Bob Block, being a close friend of Stim Bullitt, arranged for the two to meet over a dinner Block hosted in March 1954. Kay remembers that Stim was "reading a book on ancient Greece. I was always interested in things Greek." They took it from there. Two weeks later, at the future site of 1125 Harvard East, Stim asked Kay to marry him.

Marriage was not the only development in Kay's new busy life in Seattle. Apart from work and her civic involvements, Kay volunteered as a teacher and counselor at the King County Youth Service Center — the jail for offenders under age 21. When Stim ramped up his second run for Congress, Kay stepped up to manage his campaign office, such as it was. "It was a mess, an old garage or gas station," she remembers, half smiling and half frowning. "Jim Wilson took one look at it and said he'd clean it up, including the bathroom. That was a big help for me." Wilson was both a friend and fellow a liberal Democrat. An assistant state attorney general, Wilson served as legal counsel to the University of Washington.

Besides politics, Kay's time that summer also went to looking after Stim's three children. Every other weekend, she and Stim cared for Ashley, age 6; Scott, 5 (now Fred Nemo); and Jill, 3. Kay

STIMSON BULLITT
for Congress

DEMOCRAT   **1st DISTRICT**

A dapper but unsuccessful candidate.

took them to parks, read books to them and made sure they felt a part of her new family. This was not an easy arrangement. The acrimony between Kizer and Stim had involved their children. As Nemo explains it, his parents used their children as pawns in their internecine battles with one another. Kay could not tell whether Kizer would deliver the kids at prearranged times. As stepmother, she had no say, no way to decide the practical things for the three children, as a mother must do on a daily basis to keep a family running smoothly. Help came from Mrs. Bullitt, who took her grandchildren every other weekend. Still, despite Kay's best efforts, the three Kizer children never felt fully a part of the Kay-Stim household. According to Jill:

> While lacking in the kind of tenderness we might have understood when we were little, Kay took care of us in practical ways that my mother lacked the interest to pursue. Doctor and dental appointments, underwear, shoes, school supplies spring to mind. And she made a day camp for us in the summer!

Meanwhile, the house architect Fred Bassetti designed was built at 1125 and was at last ready for the Bullitts to move in. Kay was pregnant while the house was under construction. So in addition to a new home, a new baby, Dorothy Churchill Bullitt, joined the family. They all moved in when Dorothy was 3 months old. "We had no furniture, no food" says Kay. "We celebrated Christmas Eve at Mrs. Bullitt's home. The next day we began the process of settling into our house [about four blocks from her mother-in-law's home on Federal Avenue East]." Kay was now a mom times four. The family needed more room. Two additional bedrooms were added on to the east side of the house.

Concerts, meetings and ...

Kay's home soon became a center for activity, and music was part of it. Among the first performances at 1125 was a concert by the Henry Siegl Quartet, led by the Seattle Symphony's concertmaster. Siegl still was relatively new in town, having come at the behest of Milton Katims, the new symphony conductor. Among a list of impressive credits, Siegl had played with the NBC Symphony and served as

Henry Siegl

Henry Siegl was a musician, first and last. A gifted violinist, even as a young man, he formed a quartet but also performed in trios and quintets. He was concertmaster of the Seattle Symphony for 26 years, as well as for the Seattle Opera and Pacific Northwest Ballet, which were established later.

Siegl and his fellow musicians played not only in and around Seattle, but in other venues around the country. Following his death in January 1997, his son, Zev, told *The Seattle Times*' Melinda Bargreen, "He took his music every place he could, until well after he was really able to do it. He loved to take out his violin for kids and show them how the instrument was made and played, and tell them about famous players and musicians of the past. He gave audiences plenty to think about."

Looking back in the winter of 2013, Zev said, "My father was tireless about donating his services to young people, old people and community groups of all kinds. Henry loved being with people. He loved chamber music — really played chamber music all his life."

concertmaster for George Balanchine's New York City Ballet. It was in New York that Siegl and Katims had met and performed together.

An early political gathering of liberal Democrats at 1125 was "witnessed" by the 2-year-old daughter, Lindsay, of Bullitt friends Ken and Elinor McDonald. The McDonalds had taken their older daughter to Boston for surgery. Kay agreed to watch the toddler. As the 20 or so Democrats discussed their business over lunch, little Lindsay remained happily in her crib in the living room.

As an alumna, Kay also kept up her ties to Radcliffe. She hosted a tea at her mother-in-law's for scholarships sponsored by the

Kay chats with Cynthia Spring (at center), Bellevue High School, winner of a Mount Holyoke scholarship, and Alice Henderson, Roosevelt High School, winner of a National Merit Scholarship to Radcliffe College.

Photo courtesy of the *P-I* Collection, MOHAI.

Seven [Sisters] College Conference, an event featured in the *Seattle Post-Intelligencer.*

Woodrow the donkey

If anyone required proof that 1125 Harvard East was a welcoming place, the 1956 political season delivered irrefutable evidence. Friend and fellow Democrat James B. (Jim) Wilson decided to run for Congress in the 1st Congressional District. Now, Jim had an unusual pet, a donkey named Woodrow. And since the campaign would occupy most of Wilson's waking hours over the summer and fall, he asked Kay and Stim if he could park Woodrow in their spacious yard for the duration. They agreed.

There is no record of how this makeshift animal refuge conformed to city regulations. But Woodrow took up residence in the yard and was fed and watered by the family in proper fashion. When the Bullitts went up to Leavenworth, where Mrs. Bullitt had built a vacation house Copper Notch, near Icicle Creek — near today's Sleeping Lady Resort — for a few days, another friend and fellow Democrat (and later a noted King County Superior Court judge) Solie Ringold agreed to look after Woodrow. All went well until one day Woodrow kicked over his water bucket. After a while, he became thirsty and, with no water to drink, he began to bray … and bray … and bray. Neighbors complained about the racket. Wilson had to remove his pet. In the bargain, he lost the election.

One could understand if Kay shed no tears at the departure of Woodrow. She kept her focus on raising four young children. There was some time for political activities, including hosting the Democratic presidential candidate, former Illinois Gov. Adlai Stevenson. But there was not an excess of hours for many civic and social events. She was pregnant with Ben.

Former presidential candidate Democrat Adlai Stevenson visits 1125; from left, Ben on ladder by pool, Scott Bullitt (later Fred Nemo), Dorothy, Stevenson, Jill and Ashley.

Progressive green shoots: Allied Arts and Metro

Liberals Stim Bullitt and Jim Wilson did not win public office. Yet they and their friends made progress on other fronts. A group of University of Washington professors, architects and the Seattle Art Museum's art director met to discuss a civic agenda for advancing the arts. Out of this "Beer and Culture Society" came the call for a Congress of the Allied Arts, which in 1955, they incorporated as Allied Arts.

That same year, this new group persuaded the mayor and City Council to establish a Municipal Arts Commission. According to HistoryLink.org,

> One of the first products of Allied Arts and the new Art Commission was a campaign for a new civic center. Seattle voters approved $7.5 million in public bonds in November 1956 to upgrade the existing Civic Auditorium (now Opera House), which laid the financial foundation for the Seattle World's Fair six years later. Robert J. Block played a major role in these efforts, and he later guided creation of the Allied Arts Foundation, which funds small art projects and arts groups.

Bullitt friend Bob Block had, at Mayor Allan Pomeroy's request, taken charge of the bond issue that voters approved, and the civic center land was bought. Subsequently, the proposal for the City Council to appropriate $25,000 to fund a drive to sponsor a world's fair at the site was rejected. So the business community raised the money itself and the project was launched.

That same year, Allied Arts represented 57 local arts organizations and 55 leading artists and activists, including painter Kenneth

Callahan, sculptor and painter George Tsutakawa and writer Lucile McDonald.

On a much smaller scale, the organist and choirmaster at Christ Episcopal Church in the University District, John B. Andrews Jr., and his wife, Leslie, organized a performance of Gilbert and Sullivan's *The Mikado*. Kay attended the operetta on February 22, 1955. It was so successful that a second show was scheduled and the reviews were terrific. The following year, John and Leslie Andrews founded the Seattle Gilbert and Sullivan Society. Kay has been a faithful supporter ever since.

The November election of Albert D. Rosellini in 1956 put a Democrat in the governor's office, even though Washington state voted to re-elect Republican President Dwight Eisenhower for a second term. Kay was pregnant again. This time, she brought forth a boy, Benjamin Logan Bullitt, born on February 22 (Kay's birthday), 1957. The former fourth-grade teacher now had a brood of five in her charge while maintaining a busy schedule of civic activities.

Kay and Stim hosted a meeting of many of the participants in the Keechelus group as well as others to discuss how they could agitate for peace. The result, Platform for Peace, was a proposal to lobby each of the political parties to include in their respective platforms a plank that called for Democrats and Republicans alike to work for peace.

The County of King in the 1950s was fragmented into a gaggle of some 180 local governments (including Seattle), ranging in size from small towns and special service districts to the large urban center. There was virtually no cooperation or much in the way of communication among these many public agencies large and small, despite the fact the area was growing rapidly and faced the prospect of continued growth long term. Enter James R. "Jim" Ellis, a Seattle attorney whose expertise was public finance. Ellis had delivered a persuasive speech to the Seattle-King County Municipal League, of which Kay was a member, calling for a new government entity to address "metropolitan" problems, regional in nature, which spilled across jurisdictional boundaries. His ideas took hold. In 1957 the state Legislature approved an enabling law allowing a public vote only in King County that, if approved, would establish the King County-wide Municipality of Metropolitan Seattle.

The first vote, in March 1958, failed. It would have set up the new entity to manage sewage disposal and transportation. The area was suburbanizing. Plans were on the drawing board for a second Lake Washington floating bridge. While the measure passed in Seattle, it barely missed a majority in the rest of King County. That's when Mother Nature and the Block family stepped in.

The summer of '58 smelled bad. Ask anyone who lived here then. Hot weather, compounded by the area's inevitable air inversions (stagnant air trapped close to the ground) and the untreated sewage that poured into the lakes and Puget Sound, combined to cook up a foul smell that pervaded the city and its suburban neighbors. Green Lake was closed to swimming. Lake Washington was closed to swimming in both Seattle and its surrounding suburbs. Portions of Puget Sound were ruled off-limits to summertime fun too.

The Metro issue, this time authorizing only sewage treatment, was sent to the September ballot. Up stepped Dorothy Block. With her little army of five children, she organized a photograph with her youngsters standing at Matthews Beach, north of Sand Point, swimsuits donned and staring forlornly at Lake Washington next to a sign that read:

This campaign poster summed up the issue in a single picture: the combination of hot weather and stinking lakes, a wide array of endorsements political and social, and the picture power of Dorothy Block's children's brigade carried the day. The measure won by 58 percent in Seattle, 67 percent in the suburbs. Voters did want more government to clean up local waters. In time, it would do just that, and become a national model of the benefits of regional public cooperation.

Swimming or no, the big yard at 1125 provided for an interesting mix of activities. Fred Nemo, né A. Scott Bullitt, built himself "a boy's shelter" down the slope on the yard's west side, just out of sight from the house. He used the leftover debris from a demolished house (likely the one that had belonged to the Henry family) and some fallen and pruned tree branches. It was his special place. "Cigarettes and *Playboy* magazines, you know!" he recalls.

Picnics

It wasn't all "stinko" that summer of '58. While Boeing was rolling out its big, four-engine 707 airliner — to worldwide praise — Kay was rolling out her first summer picnic, in July. "I'd been driving the kids around to parks and other kinds of activities. But I wanted them to feel comfortable bringing their friends home," she says. Families came from around town and even as far away as Redmond. The picnics were potluck but Kay provided watermelons and ice cream bars. There were swings and play equipment for the kids. Adults could lounge on blankets and socialize. It was the start of something big.

People invited to the picnics included family friends and neighbors, the children's friends and schoolmates, associates of Stim's who included lawyers and mountain climbers, and Kay's colleagues active in an assortment of civic affairs. The events were social in nature, often political in fact, as the assemblage reflected the liberal, or at least liberal-leaning, people trying in some way to make Seattle a better, more progressive place. But mostly the picnics were about having fun.

Kenan Block remembers his dad's comment that "Kay's backyard was the largest private park in Seattle. Her summer picnics were ground zero for what was going on." On the patio next to the house, but overlooking the yard, there is a round table that at picnic time held a small sign marked "Reserved." That was the Bob Block table. "He had been stricken with polio and movement was difficult for him," says Kay. "He really couldn't sit on a blanket like most people who came to the picnics. So, we reserved the table for him. He enjoyed 'holding court' there."

The Siegls were regulars at the picnics. Henry always brought his violin. Zev Siegl remembers that his dad "played songs and really enjoyed entertaining: He always called it his fiddle." Kay Bullitt's July picnics would carry on to the present day. In 2008, that year's picnic celebrated a 50th anniversary. It included the grandchildren of people who had attended the gathering in the late '50s and early '60s.

The Little School

Among Kay's earliest and closest Seattle friends was Eleanor Siegl, a teacher and authority on early-childhood learning. They shared a common philosophy of education. Each was active in the field. Both were mothers of young children. They were a good match for what they were about to take on.

Together and with other friends, in coffee sessions at Kay's house, Eleanor's house and other venues, they began to form a plan to open a new preschool. "The preschools [that] operated during the war, when so many women went to work," says Kay, "were located next to the plants and factories and places of business." At war's end many were closed as the

Eleanor Siegl.

men returned and most women went back to being homemakers. "We thought there was a need for a good preschool in the neighborhoods where the families lived."

Siegl took charge. A Ph.D. who had completed her teacher training at Columbia University's Teachers College, she developed through study and teaching experience an educational philosophy congruent with what Kay believed. According to a history on The Little School's website,

> Eleanor Siegl gathered a small group of enthusiastic supporters and embarked on the courageous journey that resulted in the founding of The Little School. Along with Eleanor and Henry Siegl, the school's founding Board members were Kay Bullitt and Stimson Bullitt, Katherine and Roy Wensberg, Robert Block, and Dorothy Block.
>
> According to Dr. Siegl's progressive model, at The Little School each child would be treated as an individual. Integral

components of the school's educational environment would include students' active involvement in the learning process, development of multi-cultural awareness, and respect for others. Her goal was to move children out from behind their desks, unfold their hands, open their minds, and allow them to learn in their own ways and in their own time.

"We needed a location near a residential area," recalls Kay. "We found one at the Unitarian Church at Northeast 65th Street and 35th Avenue Northeast." The school was an immediate success. It won certification from the Washington state Board of Education in 1962. Elementary grades were added in an expansion program in 1964. A large gift enabled The Little School to buy a 10-acre site in Bellevue, where it built a new campus in 1968. Later, the school expanded in Renton. Eleanor Siegl remained the school's director until she retired in 1988. The following year, a new library and learning center were named in her honor.

The end of the 1950s found the Bullitt family growing and Seattle a changing place. The city was still run by the business-Republican elite. But, palpable forces for change — political, social and physical — were in play.

A controversial interstate freeway (I-5) was inexorably plowing through Seattle's downtown core, carving a slice from the western slope of Capitol Hill — about five blocks below 1125 — and then spanning the Lake Washington Ship Canal over an imposing high-level bridge. On the ground, green shoots of liberalism, be they the Metropolitan Democrats, Allied Arts, the bipartisan contingent of leaders who promoted and established Metro as a regional agency with an environmental agenda, had taken root and spawned a wider acceptance among what presidential candidate John F. Kennedy would describe as a "new generation" of Americans.

Mascha Siegl teaches guitar to a couple
of day-campers.

Chapter 5

Turning the corner

Obtaining the support of prominent political,
business and religious leaders demonstrated
that the liberal Democrats, in this case women
liberal Democrats, could move effectively
along the corridors of power.

As with many other places in the United States, the 1960s in Seattle
would be a decade of turmoil and change, of some awful tragedies
and some long-sought triumphs. In the lexicon of *Hair*, a smash-hit
Broadway musical depicting the new-age generation of flower
children, the Age of Aquarius produced a mixed bag for just about
everyone. Seattle did not miss out.

Summer camps

In 1960, the Bullitt children ranged in age from 16 to 3. But the
three from Stim's first marriage would not be at 1125 for much of

the decade. Ashley spent her junior high school years boarding at Annie Wright Seminary in Tacoma, followed by high school in Switzerland. Jill also boarded at Annie Wright. For high school Jill attended The Cathedral School for Girls — now named the National Cathedral School and still all-female — in Washington, D.C. Fred attended high school at Lakeside.

The children at home kept Kay busy, nonetheless. She devised new strategies for their development and education. Taking advantage of 1125's huge yard, she organized summer camps filled with fun and educational activities. Friends of the Bullitt kids, plus the children of Stim's and Kay's friends, were invited to participate. She recruited teenagers to be counselors and instructors, including Fred and Jill. Two that first summer in 1960 were Zev, 16, and Mascha Siegl, 19. "This was not a frivolous woman," Zev says of Kay. "She hired the children of Eleanor Siegl." (Zev, with two partners, in the early '70s, would establish a new business: Starbucks Coffee).

Mascha (Siegl) Kushner remembers one of the first projects was to build a playhouse — for which Kay brought in a handyman (who also worked as a professor at the UW) to help them. "It took a while," Mascha recalls, because it was "a two-story structure." Another major feature of the 1125 summer camp was a large swimming pool. Fred Nemo remembers how Stim struggled to dig the shallow pit in which the above ground pool would sit, but he "had a heck of a time. Here was this good athlete, a rock and mountain climber in good shape, but he couldn't get that pit right." The challenge and difficulty was that the pool was meant to be shallow at one end, gradually sloping down to a depth of 8 feet. Eventually, the pool was installed successfully.

There was a swing strung from a nearby tree so the kids could swing and jump off into the pool. Nemo remembers that with

TOP: Girl contemplates a jump in the water.
University of Washington Libraries, Special Collections
(UW35773);

BOTTOM: It's a hit! And a big one!
University of Washington Libraries, Special Collections
(UW35776).

delight. For her part, Kay frowns. "I worried that one of them would jump off the swing and land on the side of the pool and hurt themselves. I told them not to jump from the swing into the pool." The smile on Nemo's face suggests that the no-jumping-off-the-swing prohibition was about as successful as the ban on booze in the 1920s.

Summer camps at 1125 meant lots of play, and playacting. Zev recalls, "There was a large drama component to the camps. We read, wore togas and other costumes — and the kids shared roles." Nemo adds that "we also made shields and swords for staged fights." There also was music. Mascha played her guitar and gave some lessons. And there was "lots of singing."

TOP: Dressed in togas, summer-camp kids got to learn by taking part in Greek plays.

BOTTOM: On the wall leading down to 1125's basement, the slightly faded paintings of one summer camp's artists.

Badminton, a baseball diamond, a tree house, even tennis, games of tag and games invented on the spot were in the mix too. There were even "applied arts." Zev remembers, "We got the engine out of a wrecked car and took it apart just to see what was inside." Mascha says, "Kay had us discover [explore] the lot, the foundation of what was there before." That could have been from the home the Henrys lived in. Whatever it was, the operating principal of Kay's summer camp, in this first year and in the years to come, would always be to give children the opportunities to explore and to discover; in other words, to develop curiosity and use their imaginations. Fred, Ashley and Jill, even though they went away for school, spent most summers at 1125.

"I thought the balcony was going to collapse"

As 1961 began, with Democrat John F. Kennedy preparing to take the presidential oath of office, concerns over developments in Vietnam far away in Southeast Asia drew the interest of Kay and many of Seattle's progressive Democrats. Pregnant with their third child, she and Stim continued their political/civic activities apace. They invited Dr. W. Stull Holt, a military historian and former chairman of the University of Washington's Department of History, and U.S. Sen. Henry Jackson to conduct an evening's discussion on Vietnam.

The January event drew a larger-than-expected crowd to 1125. "I thought the balcony was going to collapse," Kay recalls. "Our house was packed!" She estimates that "some 200 people came," including alums of the Keechelus (Platform for Peace) conferences, newer members of the Metropolitan Democrats, friends and students eager to see and hear two experts take on a not very well (at the time) understood issue. Holt presented a skeptic's view regarding U.S. military involvement in this former French colony. The hawkish Jackson offered a case for confronting what he considered to be Soviet- and Chinese-sponsored communist expansion there.

Dorothy Block

Dorothy Block had been one of Kay's earliest and best friends. So it was like a stunning bolt of lightning that morning when a phone call delivered the news that Dorothy was dead. Despite the shock and pain, Kay dropped all she was doing, hurried over to the Block house and stepped in to help Bob and the kids: fixing breakfast, making sure they got off to school, taking phone calls from equally anguished friends and well-wishers. Dorothy's death blew a hole in Kay's life and the lives of the Block family she loved. "I knew Bob would be devastated," Kay recalls in a somber voice, her face (despite the years that had passed) reflecting a deep loss. "And besides, he couldn't move around easily. They needed help. It was the best thing I could do."

Dorothy Block had been part of Kay's arrival in Seattle. She and Bob engineered Kay's introduction to Stim. Kay and Dorothy shared the same frame of reference regarding life and family and civic affairs.

In a biographical note on Dorothy Block, filmmaker Ann Hedreen captured the essence of this sense of civic duty:

> "Intelligent citizen action" was what Dorothy Block was all about. A catalyst in the campaign to establish Metro, a tireless dynamo on the Seattle Park Board, a citizen advocate active in dozens of causes and projects, Block had recently given birth to her sixth child when she died following surgery

to remove a brain tumor in 1961. She was 35 years old. Her death stunned the city at a juncture in its history when the volunteer involvement she exemplified was transforming Seattle from a sleepy provincial outpost to the kind of place *Look* magazine wanted the country to know about: forward-thinking, dynamic, conservation-minded in the most modern ways.

Hedreen's use of the phrase "intelligent citizen action" came from *Look* magazine (no longer published), which presented Metro its All-American City award for 1959 for the campaign to clean up Lake Washington. *Look*'s award celebrated Dorothy Block's role in the campaign on a national stage. Hedreen's profile adds depth and dimension:

> Block wanted all citizens, not just an elite few, to embrace and enjoy Seattle's parks. She was "extremely sensitive to social imbalances" and "alert to community needs," is how columnist Douglass Welch described her in a *Seattle P-I* tribute. "Everything that touched the welfare of people and the good of the community was Dorothy's personal concern," said Rabbi Raphael H. Levine. She "abhorred the exclusive, she endured the restrictive," Rev. Peter Raible concurred. Through all of the work she did, this dedication to equality was a common thread. Among her many other commitments, Block was Vice Chairman for the Washington State Committee for the 1960 White House Conference on children and youth and vice president of the state chapter of the League of Women Voters. Block believed in the responsibility of every citizen to make sure that a city serves everyone, rich or poor. She believed that parks were a critical expression of that.

The help Kay Bullitt provided that awful morning was not forgotten by the Block family, nor were the Blocks forgotten by

Kay. They would continue to be part of 1125's picnics and summer camps as the years passed by. They would share political agendas as political campaigns came and went. They would be friends down to this very day.

Margaret

Margaret Muller Bullitt arrived on July 14, 1961. The Bullitt brood now numbered six. That her nativity coincided with the 172nd anniversary of the storming of the Bastille in Paris, and the beginning of the French Revolution, may have been a coincidence. She nevertheless joined a family bent on changing the order of things. Margaret would be the last of Kay and Stim's children.

Margaret's birth required Kay to remain in the hospital for several days. So little Jill, age 9, helped a lot to care for baby Margaret, "changing her diapers, feeding her," remembers Dorothy, who was 5 at the time. Jill was not alone caring for Margaret. Ruth Bullitt, wife of Stim's cousin Logan Bullitt, directed Margaret's care. Ruth was a trained nurse and her skills and experience came in handy. This is not to detract from Jill's contributions. Says Dorothy: "Jill was marvelous. She was the caregiver until Mother came home."

Dear Mr. President

Another close friend of Kay's, Jean Walkinshaw, shared the same passion for peace. Kay had visited war-ravaged Germany and Jean had visited atom-bomb-flattened Hiroshima. The Cold War was in full swing, so Seattle's liberals were determined to do something to counter what many feared would become World War III. The news of the day included nuclear bomb tests, tensions along the

With mother Kay attending, little Margaret entertains her grandmothers, Dorothy S. Bullitt and Marion Churchill Muller.

Iron Curtain dividing Europe between East and West, war between the Communist North Vietnam and pro-Western South Vietnam — problems that held the prospect of sucking in the United States. Kay and Jean organized a group to promote peace.

Jean and her husband, Walter Walkinshaw, Stim's boyhood friend and law partner, lived on north Capitol Hill just a few blocks from 1125. It was an easy walk for Jean, once the kids were off to school, to Kay's house to plan a peace venture over coffee. The fruit of their efforts appeared in *The Seattle Times* on November 15, 1961. It was a large half-page advertisement running the length of the page that presented

An Open Letter to the President:
WE JOIN YOU IN THE RACE FOR PEACE

The text of the missive listed five areas in which the signatories called for the president's action: war, disarmament, nuclear testing, the United Nations and Berlin. Among the 22 prominent citizens signing were Mayor Gordon S. Clinton; Dr. Solomon Katz, provost (head of the faculty) of the UW; the Rev. Samuel McKinney, pastor of Mount Zion Baptist Church; Tak Kubota of Seattle's Kubota Garden; Rabbi Jacob Singer of Temple B'nai Torah; Mrs. A. Scott Bullitt; Henry Siegl; Methodist Church Bishop Everett W. Palmer; Bagley Wright; and business leaders D.E. "Ned" Skinner II and George H. Weyerhaeuser.

Obtaining the support of prominent political, business and religious leaders demonstrated that in this case liberal women Democrats could operate effectively along Seattle's corridors of power. For Kay and Jean, this civic-action success presaged Walkinshaw's rise to becoming a nationally distinguished and award-winning television producer (KCTS Channel 9) and Kay's ascent to civic leadership both in Seattle and on the world stage.

Meanwhile, a petition made the rounds calling for the end of nuclear weapons testing. Some 3,500 people signed it, including Kay and Stim Bullitt, along with members of the city councils in both Seattle and Tacoma. Conveniently, state Rep. Dave Sprague and Bob Block were headed to Moscow on a trip to arrange art exhibits for the upcoming Century 21 World's Fair. As Anne Stadler, then executive secretary of Platform for Peace, remembers it, "They took some petitions but didn't know what to do with them, to whom they should deliver them. So they just left them on the ground in Red Square."

For her part, Anne took some of the signed petitions off to Washington, D.C. She and her husband, David, a physician teaching genetics at the UW, had returned from England, where Anne also was active in the peace movement. Dr. Stadler had helped draft the petition's language. Anne presented copies of the petitions to Arthur Schlesinger Jr., Kay's old boss in her pre-Seattle ADA days in Boston, who had become a special assistant to President Kennedy. Later, she presented more petitions to officials at the Soviet Embassy in Washington, D.C., where she engaged them during a cordial three-hour meeting. Articles in both *The Washington Post* and *The Washington Daily News* reported on Stadler's visits with Schlesinger and officials at the Soviet Embassy.

King Broadcasting

By the early '60s, King Broadcasting stood out as a solid business enterprise. Mrs. Bullitt had built it. She chose good people to manage it and to attune it to the needs of the community, the entire community. The company included television stations — KING 5 in Seattle (1949), KGW in Portland (1956), KREM in Spokane (1957) — as well as several radio stations. Mrs. Bullitt ran it. She expected the stations to make money. They did. By 1961, she was ready to back away. She did that too, but only to a point. Retaining her position as chairman of King Broadcasting's board of directors, she "asked" her son Stim to take over the presidency, to run the company. Stim agreed, although he did not particularly care for broadcasting.

HistoryLink.org quotes Stim's son, Fred Nemo: "Daddy hated the product of television, and felt that it was intellectually empty and that its influence outran its content." His younger sister Harriet told History.Link.org that "he was kind of forced into the broadcasting business. He was the man in the family, and he wanted to succeed … he saw a challenge of doing world-changing things rather than loving the business."

Finally, the website observes that,

> He settled into an unassuming windowless office, closed
> the door, and pondered the future of the world. Unlike his
> mother, and unlike his successor Ancil Payne (1921-2004),
> he tended to manage by memo and never schmoozed in the
> KING coffee shop.

And yet, "painfully shy" Stim Bullitt would make a difference. Writes HistoryLink.org: "Stim Bullitt was one of TV's first executives to hire women and African Americans [to appear on-air]. He started *Seattle* magazine, staffed it with Ivy Leaguers, and watched it scald local institutions from the Downtown Seattle Association to Broadmoor" (a chichi gated neighborhood, a rarity in the region, as was the far more affluent Highlands, where he grew up). A liberal Democrat now sat in the captain's chair of Seattle's number-one broadcasting outlet. Stim could not obtain political office. But from his office as president of King Broadcasting, he could shake the world of politics.

Century 21

It was a very big deal. Even the skeptics would come to admit that. And it made money. The Seattle World's Fair opened April 21, 1962. What in 1955 had been Allied Arts' idea for a new civic center, that spring day witnessed nothing less than a triumph for Seattle's business and political establishment with the help of many, many others. Kay volunteered at the United Nations exhibit, organized by Stim's cousin by marriage, Pat Baillargeon, and designed pro bono by 1125's architect, Fred Bassetti. Up at 1125, Kay hosted an event for an Iraqi envoy. Visitors from abroad enjoyed short stays at her house. It was a busy time. She did not host a summer camp for the kids that year. Instead, she filled the yard with a big party for her colleagues at the U.N. exhibit, visiting dignitaries, friends and family.

Century 21 changed Seattle, for the better and forever. Its legacy lives on as the Seattle Center. More than that, the World's Fair not only brought an opera company to Seattle under the leadership of Glynn Ross, it also built a new opera house for its performances, designed by the venerable architect B. Marcus ("Benny") Priteca, within the shell of the old Civic Auditorium. It's quite a list: the Space Needle, fashioned after a napkin drawing of a flying saucer in the sky; the Paul Thiry-designed Coliseum; the Play House, designed by architect Paul Hayden Kirk, which became the first home of the acclaimed Seattle Repertory Theatre (Samuel Beckett's *Waiting for Godot* played during the fair); the magnificent Minoru Yamasaki-designed Science Pavilion that now is home to the

Pacific Science Center. (Seattle-born-and-trained Yamasaki was the architect of the destroyed World Trade Center in New York City as well as Seattle's Rainier Square and IBM Buildings in the Metropolitan Tract.) Other important features from the fairgrounds include an open green whose centerpiece is a marvelous fountain big enough for kids of all ages to splash in on hot summer days and, of course, the Alweg Monorail, a Swedish promotional investment that provided swift, elevated transit from the heart of downtown's retail core to the fairgrounds in just 95 seconds — as it still does today.

An array of rides and educational entertainments for kids, booths offering a variety of international foods and cuisines, stalls of the ubiquitous souvenirs and new inventions such as direct distance dialing — there truly was something for everyone.

The nation and the world did come to Seattle. Great Britain's Prince Philip, American astronaut John Glenn (the first to circle the earth in space), Soviet cosmonaut Gherman Titov and a list of celebrities. Included were entertainers the likes of Louis Armstrong, Victor Borge, Seattle native Carol Channing, the New York City Ballet, the Canadian Tattoo and the Mormon Tabernacle Choir, all drawing sellout crowds.

The Bullitts made several visits to the fair. "We loved it," remembers Dorothy, "The rides, the exhibits, just being there. One time, Daddy gave us bus money but we — Ashley, Fred, Jill and I — walked home crossing through the construction of I-5 to save a quarter. That way we had something extra to spend."

Another Century 21 legacy, more one of attitude than of a physical manifestation, was the social liberalizing of Seattle and, to an extent, the surrounding environs. State blue laws that severely restricted the sale of alcoholic beverages and the hours bars could stay open eventually were dashed on the trash heap of Victorian morality by public vote in 1966. Ragingly popular at the fair were Gracie Hansen's adults-only Paradise International, where tastefully topless dancers pranced à la Las Vegas, and *Les Poupées de Paris*, a hilarious adults-only puppet show. Filmed at the fair was a successful Elvis Presley movie, *It Happened at the World's Fair*, which, in turn, showcased the city as an inviting backdrop for Hollywood moviemaking. Easier drinking, risqué entertainment, later bar hours, national attention, in combination with all the hoopla, opened Seattle's eyes to a looser and more sophisticated lifestyle.

At the fair's opening, *Life* magazine did a cover story on the six-month-long event. Century 21 enjoyed big play in *The New York Times* and news outlets all across the country. Seattle basked in and learned about the value of major attention from the media. When the fair shut down on October 21, 1962, just short of 10

million visitors had come to see it, and the event actually posted a profit. Not in the political sense as much as in the values sense, the Seattle World's Fair produced a liberalization of the city. It had cast itself in a show on the world stage and played its part very well. The provincial port city that Kay Muller had moved to nine years earlier was no longer. In a polite and discernible way, Seattle's many post-World War II newcomers like Kay Bullitt had helped it grow up.

Now the city was possessed of a more expanded, more mature worldview. Just as travel can be broadening and can open one's mind and heart to different peoples and places, the World's Fair broadened Seattle's attitudes in ways that eroded old prejudices and proclivities. Not all at once, mind you. There was yet much to be done. But the soil here had been tilled anew and fertilized by the fair in ways that would not have happened without Century 21. A social and cultural liberalizing had taken root. These developments caused by the fair generated an inspirational wind at the backs of political progressives whose influence and successes would increase.

Green shoots no longer

A month before Century 21 opened, another liberalizing development resulted from a green shoot of the previous decade. In 1956, as president of the Metropolitan Democratic Club, attorney Ken MacDonald wrote a letter to a Chinese-American UW student, Wing Luke, a Young Democrat, inviting him to join the MDC. Luke joined. By March 1961, he was a candidate for the Seattle City Council. His victory and that of Lud Kramer, a progressive Republican, marked a turning point in city politics. Both young men brought new energy and an openness to change to the stodgy narrowness that marked the council's other seven members.

Luke's election not only delivered the first ethnic minority to the City Council. It also symbolized an electoral acceptance of the Chinese-American community that historically had been badly mistreated by official Seattle. Once he took his seat, according to HistoryLink.org,

> Luke quickly distinguished himself as a champion of
> civil rights, progressive reform, and urban conservation.

[Architect] Victor Steinbrueck … credited Luke with sparking the movement that saved the Pike Place Market. For his part, … [New York-born] Kramer supported efforts by fellow council member Wing Luke to enact an open housing law banning racial discrimination in housing.

Kramer may not have been part of the Stevenson-MDC crowd. But he represented other moderate, progressive Republicans who would work with Democratic colleagues to improve the community. His election, alongside Luke's, served to ratify progressive values that were not in vogue a decade earlier.

The civil rights movement, led nationally by the Rev. Dr. Martin Luther King Jr., Roy Wilkins and James L. Farmer Jr., gained in credibility, popularity and solidarity in 1960s Seattle. Dr. King's "I have a dream speech" galvanized people of goodwill all across America. In Seattle, the Rev. Samuel B. McKinney at Mount Zion Baptist Church and the Rev. Dr. John H. Adams, pastor of the First African Methodist Episcopal Church, stood out as vocal and articulate leaders of the civil rights movement. They were backed by the Bullitts, the Blocks, the MacDonalds, the entire phalanx of Metropolitan Democratic Club members, plus a growing number of friends and colleagues who continued a determined, unrelenting advocacy for an end to racial discrimination. Kay found her role at the neighborhood level.

The downer, of course, was the assassination of President Kennedy in Dallas on November 22, 1963. Like so many people across the nation, the Bullitts stayed glued to their black-and-white television, parking themselves in 1125's kitchen, watching the events unfold. Kennedy and his brother "Bobby" had become active promoting civil rights: the president giving speeches — some of his very best — and Attorney General Bobby sending federal marshals into Southern states to protect black citizens' peaceful protests and access to the voting booths. The president's shocking death cast a palpable gloom everywhere. "We were devastated," remembers Kay, in a soft, solemn tone. The push for civil rights, nevertheless, continued apace.

The Goldmark case

Good and happy news arrived early in 1964 on the legal/political front. Family friend and fellow Democrat state Rep. John Goldmark won a lawsuit against four individuals and the *Tonasket Tribune*, a weekly newspaper in north-central Washington, which had conducted a vicious campaign smearing him with allegations of "communism" when he had run in 1962 for re-election to the state Legislature. Goldmark lost that election. The trial became a mean-spirited occasion for the plaintiffs again to attack not only Goldmark but also his wife Sally, who as a young woman had been a member of the Communist Party before moving to Washington, but who was never in sympathy with any call for the violent overthrow of the United States government. The jury's verdict delivered a significant victory for the Goldmarks, to be sure. More broadly, the verdict reinforced the liberals' position that far-right Republicans could not be trusted to serve the larger public good. It stood specifically as a condemnation of the John Birch Society in Washington state, which sought to continue the largely baseless campaign to ferret out "Communists," employing the tactics of disgraced former Republican U.S. Sen. Joe McCarthy of the previous decade.

"I don't think in this state there has ever been such an example of people going so far and acting so viciously to ruin a man's name," remarked Goldmark's attorney, William Dwyer, in the trial's closing arguments. Later that year, the case was overturned. The appellate judge said that while evidence in the case established that Goldmark was not a communist, and that the defendants had made false charges in attacking him politically, under a Supreme Court decision a public official could not collect damages when there was no proof of malice. A detailed account is available at HistoryLink.org.

In addition to the jury's verdict, the case demonstrated the tenor of the times in another important way. One of the witnesses for Goldmark was his former colleague in the state Legislature, Republican Rep. Slade Gorton of northeast Seattle, who would go on to serve as Washington's attorney general and eventually as one of its U.S. senators. Gorton stood among a significant number of Republicans then who not only rejected the McCarthyite tactics of right-wingers but also were willing to work with Democrats to achieve commonly shared goals — in this instance, political comity and a more congenial civil society.

Although the Goldmarks continued to own their ranch in eastern Washington's Okanogan Valley, they moved to Seattle, where John would practice law. They lived at 1125 while they looked for a house to buy.

Open housing

The push for civil rights resulted in an open-housing referendum placed before Seattle voters on March 10. The campaign manager was Stim's childhood friend and distant relative, Pat Baillargeon. The day before the balloting, the campaign placed a full-page ad in *The Seattle Times* headlined with the call for

Equal Opportunity for Housing
IT'S UP TO YOU

So many people signed the ad that their names appeared in tiny print below it. Among them was Mrs. Stimson (Kay) Bullitt.

Unhappily, Seattle's (overwhelmingly white) voters were not ready to advance a more congenial civil society. They voted down the referendum almost two to one. Local real estate interests had mounted a hard-hitting campaign with advertisements. According to HistoryLink.org, "One ad proclaimed, 'Your Rights are at Stake! Would you like a criminal record because you sold your home or rented your apartment to a person of your choice?' " This defeat for liberals — City Council members Luke and Kramer had pushed hard for passage — did not deter Kay Bullitt.

Just about the same time, the two Democrats on the three-member King County Board of Commissioners, Ed Munro and Scott Wallace, approved an open-housing bill. The *P-I* reported in its March 10 editions that kingpin GOP County Prosecutor Charles O. Carroll announced he would not enforce it, that it had been changed from the bill initially advertised. That was Carroll's legal fig leaf, meant to cover his opposition to open housing and his support for the real estate interests who also stood in opposition.

Summer camp: New and improved

Meanwhile, Kay's camp at 1125 that summer of '64 advanced the ball for her civil rights agenda. She integrated the camp. "It was right after the March on Washington and people were exercised about the schools," Kay said to Paula Bock, of *The Seattle Times*. "The kids enjoyed sharing their experiences. We had a baseball backstop in those days, a stand-up pool. I did Greek tragedies, and

Counselor and camper focus intently on a book. From University of Washington Libraries, Special Collections (UW 35775).

some parents taught music, and Betty Jane Narver taught Chinese calligraphy."

Kay invited the minority children of friends and acquaintances, making sure they were included and enjoyed the same fun and educational experiences as their Caucasian counterparts. Stim had built a rope swing and a tree house with an open front. Kids could enter the elevated structure by using the rope swing to swing their way inside. "It was a very popular feat," remembers Dorothy. Kids tried and, with a bit of practice, succeeded in getting the timing and arc of their swing just right to land them in the tree house.

Badminton, croquet and other assorted games — some invented on the spot — helped to fill out the menu of activities. A large old cargo net was hung from trees over on the west side. The kids climbed on it like little commandos. Quiet times also played a role at the summer camp sessions. There were board games, art projects and periods for reading.

The glee of the camp that summer dampened the afternoon of August 2. Margaret and friend Kayla Black were playing at the house. Kay had turned on the radio and soon there came an ominous bulletin that the American destroyer USS *Maddox*, on patrol in the Gulf of Tonkin off the coast of Vietnam, had been attacked by North Vietnamese torpedo boats. That development, manipulated by the president, led to congressional passage of the Gulf of Tonkin Resolution. It authorized the president to aid any Southeast Asian nation that was attacked by a communist country. In effect, it gave President Johnson unlimited power to escalate the war against North Vietnam. Johnson did that. Expanding the war provoked a strong response at 1125 Harvard East and, in time, at King Broadcasting.

Back row: Ashley, Stim, Kay, Scott (later Fred) middle: Margaret in Kay's lap, Ben in front of Scott front: Dorothy, Jill

SOS

Meanwhile, Kay busied herself with another passion: historic preservation. She became involved in the work to save the Northwest's rare and disappearing ships. The dozens of phone calls to and from 1125, the coffee sessions at her kitchen table, culminated for her in

City Councilman Wing Luke smiles at the large donation to help finance preservation of the *Wawona*. Kay, lower right, and other Save Our Ships supporters look on.

Photo courtesy of Northwest Seaport.

joining a group known then as Save Our Ships, fitting well with the official international maritime distress signal SOS. It was through this endeavor that Kay linked up with City Councilman Wing Luke. She had met Luke at a party, talked with him about historic preservation and wound up convincing him to get involved with SOS.

In 1964, restaurateur Ivar Haglund joined Kay and Councilman Luke in the SOS venture. Haglund and Mrs. Bullitt together donated $27,000 to purchase the *Wawona* from a Montana rancher whose urge to haul cattle on it had passed. For the next 46 years, Kay and Haglund (while he was alive) and several others worked hard to raise the funds to restore the *Wawona*. Kay's unrelenting work to save the *Wawona* would inspire her grandson Benjamin Schmechel to write a paper on the history of the ship as an assignment for his high school history class.

Turning violent

Nationally and locally, the 1960s witnessed some important advances as well as some awful setbacks. Already there was the assassination of President Kennedy, November 22, 1963. His death led to a powerful mandate for Vice President Lyndon Baines Johnson (LBJ), who won both passage of the landmark 1964

Wawona

Launched in 1897, the *Wawona* carried full loads of lumber up and down the Pacific Coast, in her hold and on her deck, as well as loads of pilings under the foresail boom.

Below is an excerpt from

Wawona: Seattle's Floating Heritage

By Benjamin Bullitt Schmechel
7 May 2007

Out of the ever increasing demand for wood as a building material, and the newfound need of the West Coast's galloping lumber industry to transport its resource, came two sister ships, the *C. A. Thayer* and the largest three-master sailing schooner ever to be built in North America, the *Wawona*.

While the *Wawona* would one day hold great significance for the Seattle region, she began her life on September the 12th, 1897, at the H.D. Bendixen Shipyard in Fairhaven, California, built on a commission by the Dolbeer & Carson Lumber Company of Eureka, California. For the seventeen years that followed, with the decks and holds of her 165-foot-long frame stacked high with sawn lumber, she would make her way up along the Pacific coast, faithfully carrying her loads from the primeval forests of northern California to Grays Harbor and other such ports around the Northwest.

In 1914, eager to lend her hand to another major Northwest industry, the *Wawona* began her term in the cod fishing trade. Sold to the Robinson Fisheries Company of Anacortes, Washington, the *Wawona* spent her next thirty years carrying a crew of thirty-six men each spring to the Bering Sea for the six-month cod fishing season.

Civil Rights Act and election to the White House in a massive landslide of votes. Johnson also schemed to deepen America's military involvement in the war in Vietnam. Within months of his election, he sent bombers to hammer North Vietnam's cities and its infiltration and supply routes south. He ordered an enormous buildup of troops, made possible by the continuation of the World War II compulsory military draft for all young American men that would eventually exceed a half million on the ground, in the air and at sea.

Protests in the '60s that had focused on civil rights now expanded to oppose the war in Vietnam. Some protests turned violent on college and university campuses, including at the UW. There were race riots in many cities. Properties were burned, clashes with law enforcement sent protesters and police alike to hospitals, and the nation began to reel and take sides, leading to some bitter divisions, political and personal. Seattle would not escape the turmoil. The home of a liberal Democrat, state Rep. David Sprague, was firebombed while his family was there and he was away at the Capitol in Olympia. He thought it was "because he was a white legislator in an area that was predominantly black," according *The Seattle Times*. State Sen. Fred Dore's home nearby also was firebombed. He quickly moved his family to a suburb and left the Legislature, clearing the way for a former UW football star, the African-American George Fleming to take the seat. Nevertheless, Sprague (whose insurance firm counted King Broadcasting as a major client) remained in his Central Seattle-Madrona neighborhood home, continuing his vigorous advocacy for civil rights. In another despicable incident, a man posting a letter in the University District died from a bomb that exploded when he opened the mail chute to deposit his letter.

Wing Luke down

On May 17, 1965, the call that rang in at 1125 conveyed portentous news. Kay's friend and compatriot in work to save the *Wawona*, City Councilman Wing Luke, was missing. It would be a year before they located the wreckage of the plane. Luke and two others were returning from a fishing trip at Wannacut Lake in Okanogan County. An important vote involving the city's garbage-hauling contract was scheduled for the next day. The fatal crash occurred at Merchant Peak near Index in the Cascade Mountains. When the standard search parties could not locate the missing plane, Kay paid for continuation of the search herself. "I thought it was not right for him and his friends to simply be lost. We finally found them."

The lethal accident might have claimed the life of Stim's sister Harriet. She had been invited to go along via a telephone call taken by her son Scott. Fortunately, he forgot to deliver the message and the party took off without Harriet.

Luke was both well liked and respected as a young and promising political leader. He was one of two Metropolitan Democratic Club members to win office when so many others had failed. (The other was attorney Brock Adams, who won the 7th Congressional District seat in the '64 election.) Luke had fought, albeit unsuccessfully, for an open-housing law. He had served as an inspiration for others who wanted changes at Seattle City Hall.

Out with the JBS

The 1964 landslide election of President Johnson nationally and in Washington state did not coattail a Democrat into the governor's mansion in Olympia. Young Dan Evans, a Republican state legislator from Seattle — by training a civil engineer — won on his platform, a "Blueprint for Progress." Part of that blueprint would redirect his own political party and set a high tone for his long tenure as the state's chief executive.

On the 10th of September, 1965, not even a year in office, the new governor dropped a bombshell that pleased progressive Democrats and most decent citizens of any political persuasion around the Evergreen State.

Addressing a gathering of state Republican leaders in Port Angeles, Evans spoke plainly:

"I do not intend to watch the destruction of our great party and with it the destruction of the American political system. Let those who are false prophets, the phony philosophers, the professional bigots, the destroyers, leave our party," declared Evans, according to *Seattle Times* reporter Lyle Burt, who covered the event.

State Republicans Repudiate 'Birch'

By LYLE BURT
Times Staff Reporter

PORT ANGELES.—Washington State Republicans today backed Republican Gov. Dan Evans and adopted a resolution repudiating the John Birch Society and similar organizations.

The resolution, drafted by the party's state executive board early this morning, was approved, 43 to 15, when it came before the full state central committee shortly before noon.

IN AN ADDRESS to the central committee last night, Evans denounced the John Birch society and asked its members to leave the Republican party.

Approval of the document was the culmination of a long-festering dispute within party ranks over the ence of Birch bers of

the closed-door meeting said only two "no" votes were heard.

Arguments which blocked an earlier conclusion of the resolution - writing session centered around whether to name the John Birch Society or whether to refer only to "extremists."

State Chairman C. Montgomery Johnson had insisted that the Birch Society be named.

JOHNSON expressed confidence that the full Central Committee will give its approval to the document.

Generally, the resolution sets forth a series of tests which an organization should meet to be acceptable to the Republican conclu

Republican officials then worked long into the next morning, according to Burt, drafting a statement following up on the governor's speech. In part it read:

Such groups as the John Birch Society demonstrate by their methods, their leadership and their policies that they fail to meet the tests and to follow the traditions of the Republican Party.

They do not contribute to its victory, but to its defeat. They do not strengthen it, but weaken it. They do not effectively promote conservative principles; they subvert them.

The GOP's executive board, by a vote of 43-15, approved the statement the next day. The John Birchers, the ones who had tried to use the legal system to lynch the Goldmarks, were officially invited out of the Republican Party. In the course of two days, Dan Evans had reshaped the GOP and set a course for political comity that would guide his years in elective office. With help from enough of the state's Democrats, he would be the only governor in Washington's history to serve three terms.

That Evans and most in his party, were willing to stand up to the John Birchers spoke well of the mid-'60s, when many Republicans and Democrats sought to work together. In a state with no party registration, with a unique "blanket primary" allowing voters to choose whatever candidate they fancied in a primary election, candidates needed to reach across party lines and to independents. Each side had its extreme partisans. Each side would fight the other intensely. Yet both would try to find common ground on important issues. Sometimes they would reach compromise; other times not. But they shared an ethic of leadership that aimed at making things better. In a word, they were willing to work toward compromise.

Kay and Stim made a trip abroad that year. They toured the Mediterranean, taking the opportunity to get away, just as a couple. Years later, Kay would return to the area, spending time in Israel and Palestine, visiting the family of her friend the playwright Nogarus Sainai and a Palestinian man who was building a K-12 school. On a return trip years later, she saw the completed school, which was integrated with both Palestinian and Jewish children.

A shy man's editorial

Up on Harvard East, the kids were growing up. The summer camps drew more children. Kay's July picnics kept pace as new friends joined the regulars, whose own families expanded. Politics and social issues were never far off the radar screen at the Bullitt home. Kay volunteered at the children's schools, chiefly Lowell Elementary four blocks away, later at Meany Middle School. Stim presided in a most quiet and inconspicuous fashion down the hill at King Broadcasting on Dexter Avenue North.

Stim, however, had not been inconspicuous at home or with close friends about his concerns over the escalation of American involvement in Vietnam: Bombing raids north, more and more troops being committed to battle, the sickening pictures and growing numbers of body bags containing dead U.S. soldiers and Marines on the evening news programs carried by his television stations weighed heavily on him. He and Kay believed fervently that the American war effort was misguided. Stim decided to speak out.

December 23, 1966, on KING TV in Seattle, KGW in Portland and KREM in Spokane, Bullitt personally went on the air and delivered an editorial he had written — and rewritten, according to Kay — stating, "The intensity of our military action should be stepped down, and we should stop bombing North Vietnam."

Bullitt argued that the U.S. should keep troops in South Vietnam, holding our ground there. He called for the South Vietnamese "to move toward a government which is constitutional and, later, representative as it ought to be."

He concluded by saying,

And our new direction can assist us: first, to reduce the bloodshed — ours and theirs; second, to cool the overheated atmosphere of that miserable country as a step to enabling its inhabitants to make peace with each other; and last, to raise our standing among the nations and relax the tension between the great powers until they can suppress those instruments [nuclear bombs] which can, and may, wipe out the human race.

In calling for a halt to the bombing of North Vietnam, Bullitt had dropped a bomb of his own. The switchboards at all three King stations lit up with calls in both support and opposition from viewers as well as listeners who tuned to radio stations owned by King Broadcasting. Importantly, Stim's stand drew national attention and contributed to the growing momentum across America of people questioning our nation's role, especially our war-making role in Southeast Asia, in what many considered to be more a civil war than a communist threat to our country's vital interests.

One attentive listener was daughter Margaret, then 5. In his book *River Dark & Bright*, Bullitt recalls that during his editorial he had made a reference to "hostile guerrillas," "at which she jumped to her feet with shining eyes and shouted, 'Gorillas!!' "

Discussions at 1125 often included the war, its effects and politics. Three years later, Stim would deliver one more on-air editorial, this time opposing President Richard Nixon's decision to expand U.S. bombing to neighboring Cambodia. As Kay tells it,

> Stim was very upset and angry about Nixon's decision to bomb Cambodia. He wrote the editorial himself. Because of his extreme shyness, people at KING worried about his ability to effectively present the piece on-air. But he felt it was important. So he did it. He got such a positive response. He was so astounded that he was getting all this support from around the country. Mrs. Bullitt supported it.

In league

Kay's work to advance civil rights had not stopped at the integration of her educational summer camps. Nor did the defeat of the open-housing referendum impede her efforts on that front. With a KING 5 News reporter along, and with Dorothy and Ben as witnesses, she went around some Capitol Hill blocks with an African-American person trying to rent an apartment advertised as available. The responses — "Sorry, we're full up"; or "Oh, we've already rented that unit"; or "The apartment is not available" — all carried the same message: "No black person wanted here."

Kay's commitment put her views and feelings and actions on the line, at her home, in her neighborhood, around the city. This had not gone unnoticed. By 1967, she was invited to join the board of the Seattle Urban League, the only white person at the time to be so honored. She accepted. She also became a board member of the Seattle Opportunities Industrialization Center (focused on job training and education for inner-city youths) and remained a member until 1989.

With Wing Luke gone, the Seattle City Council returned to its all-white membership. But by 1967, Luke's legacy of breaking the line barring people of color and of minority ethnicity would be crossed for good. A large number of varied interests came together to form Choose an Effective City Council, CHECC for short. Progressive Democrats and Republicans, independents, some businesspeople, including some members of the Junior Chamber of Commerce, Allied Arts, League of Women Voters and many people unaffiliated stepped up to promote change. They wound up sponsoring three candidates for the council: Tim Hill, a young deputy King County prosecutor; Phyllis Lamphere, president of the League of Women Voters; and Sam Smith, a state legislator and expeditor at Boeing who was African-American. All three won.

Seattle voters not only had sent an ethnic minority to sit among its legislative body. Their City Council had become more open to changes, more progressive and less beholden to Seattle's power elite at the Chamber and Central Association. In a word, the city itself was more liberal. Those Stevenson Democrats, who had for years worked and longed for a more open and progressive community, were seeing many of their values win the day. In April the following year, six council members sponsored an open-housing ordinance. Then, civil rights leader the Rev. Dr. Martin Luther King Jr. was assassinated. Two weeks later, the open-housing ordinance won unanimous approval.

The ball of progressivism also advanced on another front, on the liberal Democrats' own playing field. Women were now allowed to join the all-men's Metropolitan Democratic Club. "For most of the things they did," Kay says, "we wives were around and involved anyway." Nevertheless, it showed that the self-proclaimed progressives themselves could make progress. "We were pleased," Kay notes.

Lucy

"Lucy came to me via my father, who received her [an infant raccoon whose mother had died] from Tom Dargan, a colleague at King," says Dorothy, who was 10 at the time. A new friendship, almost a partnership in life, was born.

At first, Lucy slept with Dorothy. But as she grew and developed over the next year, she was given a very large "bedroom-sized" cage. The yard at 1125, after all, offered plenty of room for that. Even so,

Dorothy with her pet raccoon, Lucy, next to the house at 1125.

she enjoyed companionship of which no other raccoon could boast. She swam with Dorothy. She went for walks and on bike rides and even went skiing with Dorothy. She frolicked in that big, expansive yard with Dorothy. Surely this was better treatment than Toto got from that other Dorothy in their *Wizard of Oz* adventure.

Moreover, Lucy was not above some high jinks on her own. Next door, on the north side of 1125, the Bloedels' house had been purchased by the British government for its Seattle consulate office and consular residence. As events would have it, the consul was preparing to host a visit by the prime minister of Northern Ireland — no small event.

That afternoon caterers set up a nice spread in the consulate's backyard, open to a view of Queen Anne Hill and Lake Union. Lucy must have sniffed the fact there was food next door. She was caught helping herself to the hors d'oeuvres. "We were so embarrassed. We got her back home and decided it was time to get her in a cage," remembers Kay.

"A day or so later, the phone rang. The son of the bishop at St. Mark's called to say he wondered if the raccoon in their backyard was Lucy. There was another wild raccoon in the neighborhood. But we got the cage, went two doors up the street and, sure enough, it was Lucy."

There's more. "A few days later," Kay continues, "we heard from the British consul of the thank-you note he'd received from the Irish prime minister. All it said was 'How's Lucy?' "

By the time Lucy was two, she had become aggressive, too much so for the city. Stim took Dorothy and her friend to Leavenworth so Lucy could take her natural place in the wild. "It was very hard," Dorothy says wistfully. "It was hard to let her go."

Keepin' on, keepin' on

The assassination of Dr. King left people depressed. When the same fate struck down Sen. Robert Kennedy, after a major victory in the 1968 California primary that many believed would propel him to the Democratic nomination for president, it seemed to Kay and many others that civic life might not ever be as civil as it was once or should be.

To Kay, it was not the time to back off. At a series of meetings, some at 1125, she organized a voluntary partnership program for student transfers between Lowell Elementary School, where her children attended, and Madrona Elementary School in the city's east-central neighborhood. This was an effort to improve integration. She didn't stop there. Middle-class families were abandoning Seattle and its public schools, for the perceived greener pastures and better schools in suburbia. On top of this "white flight," some of Seattle's better-prepared black students were leaving public schools for private alternatives. Kay decided that if a program to boost the quality of offerings at schools attended by central-city students could be established, their families might stay put.

Over coffee and tea at 1125, she and Gordie Albi devised a plan to bring volunteer adults with special expertise and skills into the schools to augment what teachers already were doing. With the full cooperation of principal Dan Goertzen at Madrona Elementary, the venture got under way. "He was very helpful," Kay recalls. "Space was tight. One science class was held in a closet. We also were able to use the city library across the street [eventually named for Sally Goldmark] before it opened its door at 10 in the morning. A creative writing class was held there."

There was no push-back from the Seattle Teachers Association. "I think they liked it," says Kay. "I think they supported what we were trying to do, to keep students in public schools, especially the better black students." This venture, known as the Volunteer Instruction Program, proved such a success that it spread to other schools

Steps: Some small, some large

The final year of the '60s would be indelibly remembered for astronaut Neil Armstrong's stepping onto the surface of the moon and saying for all in the world to hear: "This is one small step for a man, one giant leap for mankind." Thus did the United States of America achieve the goal set by the late President John F. Kennedy; the moon landing also opened up the space age, as had only been dreamt of over the centuries. "We all watched the moon landing in the basement," remembers Dorothy. "The television was in the basement then because Daddy did not want us to watch it." Of course, the moon landing was the exception to that rule.

Kay's sister Margie and her husband could tell a moon landing story of their own. Margie's husband, Arlan Baillie, a Congregational minister, presided at the marriage of Neil

Armstrong and his wife. The Rev. Baillie would tell his family and friends that he had touched the ring that landed on the moon.

For Kay Bullitt and the Seattleites working for harmony on earth, 1969 began on a gruesome, fearsome note.

The morning of January 26, Kay got the kids off to school, then walked over to the bus stop. She rode out to near the Seattle-Tacoma International Airport for a meeting of the Urban League. Among her colleagues there was Edwin T. Pratt, a prominent leader in the African-American community and the Urban League's executive director. Kay returned home from the meeting. Late that night, the shock came with the ring of the doorbell. At the door, a colleague told Kay that Pratt had been fatally shot just before 9 p.m. on his front porch. Kay was stunned, as was the entire — well, almost the entire — community.

Next morning, King County Sheriff Jack Porter told *The Seattle Times*, "I can see no other motivation for the killing other than politics or race." The business community immediately put up $10,000, for a reward hoping someone would provide information leading to the arrest of the three killers, seen by witnesses as they fled to a waiting car. Pratt, 38, had settled with

$10,000 Reward

Assassin Killed Pratt, Says Sheriff

A $10,000 reward was announced today for information leading to conviction of the slayers of Edwin T. Pratt, Seattle Negro leader who Sheriff Jack Porter said may have been the victim of political assassination.

Porter said the reward was offered by the business community of Seattle and King County and many friends of Pratt "as an expression of their deep concern and sorrow."

Persons with information were asked to contact the sheriff's office. The office will respect the wishes of persons who do not want their identities to be known, Porter said.

In addition, the Board of King County Commissioners offered a $500 reward.

EARLIER today the sheriff said: "I can see no motivation for the killing other than politics or race."

Pratt was shot in the doorway of his Richmond Highlands home at 8:55 p.m. yesterday.

Deputy —

EDWIN T. PRATT
(See Page B for another photo)

wearing three-quarter-length coats. The coats may have been identical.

"THEY LOOKED like kids," he said. "They were young. It was the way they ran — the gait."

The description of the car was based on information from another witness.

The second witness told detectives he heard the shot, then watched two men run to the car and enter on the passenger side. He said they appeared to be sh— tall his wife and children in a white suburban neighborhood just north of the city, as part of an initiative to broaden housing options for minorities. He was widely respected and counted on to help improve relations between the races in Seattle, to play a major role in the leadership not only in the black community, but also on the broader stage of city affairs. His senseless death left a hole in the city's civic leadership. His murderers have never be caught.

Face to Face

The assassination of Ed Pratt occurred during a larger, sometimes direct and often bluntly spoken dialogue on race relations in Seattle. Helping lead this was a television program on Stim Bullitt's Channel 5: *Face to Face*. The program was hosted, led really, by the outspoken educator Roberta Byrd Barr, the first African-American woman to become a high school principal for Seattle Public Schools.

It is important to recall that this was a period in American history when civil rights issues remained on the front burners of many U.S. cities. There were riots, stretched tensions between police and ethnic minorities, and anger over individual slights both real and perceived. Barr took on hot topics and told it like she saw it. Producer of Barr's *Face to Face* programs was Kay's friend Jean Walkinshaw. Kay had been instrumental in Walkinshaw's hiring at King Broadcasting. And she was a friend of Barr's as well, and remained so until her death in 1993. *The Seattle Times'* Lily Eng wrote an extensive obituary on Barr that included the following observation:

> "She was very outspoken and passionate about what she believed in," said [Jean] Walkinshaw, who produced "Face to Face" and was a close friend. "She was abrasive to some and

brutally honest to others. She woke up the community to all kinds of things that had been overlooked."

Face to Face aired on KING 5 from 1965 to 1970. The program included some segments produced in the field but it was Barr's no-nonsense in-studio interviews that set *Face to Face* apart.

Sometimes her guests pulled back from her hardball questions. A rainbow of guests from ethnic minority communities included Northwest Native Americans, unusual in that day. Moreover, *Face to Face* addressed hot topics, subjects very few broadcast outlets would allow on their air, including poverty and welfare, education and desegregation, the drug scene, women's issues, housing conditions, even divorce and prostitution. It was the time of President Lyndon Johnson's Great Society.

Roberta Byrd Barr, 1919-1993.

According to *The Seattle Times'* obituary:

"She held my feet to the fire and kept them there," said Forbes Bottomly, who was school superintendent from 1965-73, during some of the most explosive racial times in the Seattle district. There were sits-in and walk-outs and disturbing questions about discrimination.

Bottomly appointed Ms. Byrd vice principal at Franklin High School after 150 students held a sit-in in March 1968, to protest the expulsion of black female students who wore their hair natural.

It may seen strange in the age of Twitter, Facebook, Instagram and other high-tech, semi-communication Internet technologies, but people in the '60s received their news from the papers, magazines, radio and television. Barr built an audience and influenced the talk and the agenda in Seattle. Perhaps it is a measure of just how effective Barr was that Pacific Northwest Bell provided a grant so the show could move to Seattle's public television station, KCTS Channel 9, where, according to Walkinshaw, "we got a better time slot." *Face to Face* appeared on KCTS for two years, in 1971 and 1972.

Fully funding public schools: Not!

The tragedy of Pratt's murder dampened spirits even as it sparked a deeper resolve to continue the work bettering race relations. For Kay this meant additional work in education. She and then-King County Superior Court Judge Charles Z. Smith were elected as co-chairs of the Parent-Teacher Association at Meany Junior High. Dorothy had attended, Ben was currently attending and Margaret would follow shortly.

Because "we needed the Legislature to fully fund the public schools," Kay joined the walk to the state Capitol in Olympia to prod elected officials to allocate more money. "We were trying to prevent white flight, trying to hold families at Meany — the good black students were going out under voluntary busing." No more then than today has the Legislature been able, or willing, to fully fund the state's public schools, court orders to do so notwithstanding.

Work in the schools did not hinder the work of educating and having fun at home. The small stage in the basement at 1125 continued to support the kids' informal plays and games. Of course, Ashley, 21 and Jill, 18, were away at school. Fred, age 20, had moved out. Dorothy, 14, Ben 12, and Margaret, 8, who had become seriously involved in ballet, comprised the remaining junior members at 1125.

Another large step, this one on Earth, occurred when Stim left
the presidency of King Broadcasting to return to the practice of law.

The short version of his departure is summed up by noting that
Stim's mother and sisters had become alarmed that his investments
and ventures at King were draining advertising revenues, in some
cases causing advertisers to pull away. He had started *Seattle*
magazine, a high-quality monthly of hard-hitting reporting, good
writing and first-rate features and photography. The magazine, in
the words of HistoryLink.org, "scald[ed] local institutions from the
Downtown Seattle Association to Broadmoor," a gated, chichi golf
club community in the east-central part of Seattle. He started King
Screen Productions, a film division that produced the Oscar-winning
The Redwoods. But both the magazine and the film operation lost
money and significantly drained the employee profit-sharing plan,
created by King Broadcasting in lieu of pensions.

His editorial opposing the bombing of North Vietnam sprang
from his keen sense that a television station should serve the public
interest. This led the King news stations to cover topics other
broadcasters would shy away from, to produce documentaries and,
on a daily basis, to meet a high standard of journalistic integrity.

Moreover, and perhaps most important, Stim Bullitt hired
women and African-Americans at KING 5.

Barbara "Bobbie" Stenson was the first woman on-air news
reporter hired at Seattle's KING TV. "Mrs. Bullitt was on the Board
of Regents at the University of Washington," Stenson recalls, adding,

> It was 1964 and she read some of my stuff when I was editor
> of *The Daily*, the UW student newspaper, and liked it. She
> took me out to dinner at Trader Vic's to sound me out and
> had the station fly me to Spokane for an interview at KREM.
> But nothing came of it, so I took a great short-term daily

newspaper job offered to me immediately on graduation.
Only a few weeks later Stim called me on the phone and said
I had a job in the KING TV news department at union scale
— higher than newspaper pay — and he would hold it for me
until I could complete my contract at the end of the year. I
suspect he'd gotten a call from his mother.

Stenson and a number of other able young journalists joined
King Broadcasting's stations in Seattle, Portland and Spokane
during that era, winning professional honors and top ratings for
their work.

According to HistoryLink.org, "His sisters and mother eased
Stim Bullitt out of King's presidency. They feared that operations
like the magazine and film company were bleeding the broadcast
operation." Talented staff began leaving the station. Ratings
slipped.

Stim took it in good humor. In his memoirs, quoting President
Abraham Lincoln, he wrote that "I felt like the man who was
run out of town on a rail and when asked how he felt about it,
said, 'Except for the honor of the thing, I'd just as soon have
walked.' Well, I would just as soon have walked six months later."
Nevertheless, as Kay remembers that time, "Stim's departure from
King darkened the mood around the house."

Around the corner and down "our" street

That November, once all the ballots were tallied, Seattle voters led
their city government down a new street. Democrat Wes Uhlman,
the youngest mayor in the city's history, at age 34, defeated his
establishment-backed opponent, former GOP legislator Mort
Frayn, by an astonishing two-to-one margin. Predictably, *The Seattle*

Uhlman Says He'll Be Cautious

BY SHELBY SCATES
P-I Political Writer

Seattle took a new departure Tuesday, electing young Wes Uhlman mayor instead of R. Mort Frayn. It turned away from leadership offered by the downtown business community toward a fresh, self-starting, political comer. It did so overwhelmingly.

Election Analysis

Voters had ratified four of the previous five candidates for mayor running with the blessing and the financial backing of downtown businessmen. Not Tuesday.

They were celebrating that fact early yesterday in a suite at the top of the splendid Washington Plaza. The mayor-elect held court in a corner. Around him new faces outnumbered the empty champagne bottles. Some were black.

For the anointment of a major political victory, it was strikingly sober. You might have expected the Mets dressing room after the World Series. What one got was political post mortems and a sense of relief.

Uhlman politely laughed off a gushing matron who suggested "you will run for governor in 1972."

He got down to business when a reporter asked him — not facetiously — if he would be as cautious a mayor as he was during his general election campaign.

His answer: "Yes."

Times had enthusiastically endorsed Frayn, branding Uhlman as "slick" and accusing him of "misleading the electorate."

For its part, the *Post-Intelligencer* issued a dual endorsement, saying both likely would do a good job. Obviously, the voters preferred Uhlman. But the endorsements signaled a shift in sentiment at the *P-I* editorial board. Seattle was about to gain an editorial page no longer lockstep conservative.

Uhlman's landslide victory delivered an unmistakable mandate for change. The Democratic state senator came from the city's working-class 32nd Legislative District — the University District-Wallingford-Ravenna area. His victory would set the course for 48 uninterrupted years of Democrats elected to the city's highest office. Uhlman hailed from the coastal mill town of Aberdeen. He graduated from the UW both as an undergrad and as a lawyer. His elevation to the Municipal Building signaled, brightly, the end of the old order.

During his eight years in office, Uhlman would aggressively promote civil rights, including the integration of the police and fire departments, halt City Light's effort to build a nuclear power station on Kiket Island in Skagit County, promote historic preservation, most notably of Pioneer Square, and the arts, particularly the establishment of Bumbershoot, the music festival held each Labor Day weekend. He would greatly expand the city's parks — with the powerful help of Senator Magnuson — including Magnuson

Park (formerly Sand Point Naval Air Station) and Discovery Park (formerly Fort Lawton).

Choosing a new mayor was not the end of it. Voters also put four newcomers on the City Council, including Chinese-American Liem Tuai. Although *The Seattle Times* of November 5, 1969, proclaimed flatly that the new City Council would be "far more liberal than the present Council," those four '69ers would turn out to be the more conservative, establishment-oriented bloc as the years unfolded.

Two CHECC candidates had lost: Robert "Bob" Block and environmentalist and lawyer Joan Thomas. Still, the old guard was out and the momentum was with the liberals — even if it would take the new mayor some time and some bumps in the road along the way to that realization.

Frayn was a good man. He owned a printing company. He was open to some changes. But when the two candidates stood side-by-side, voters could see the youthful Uhlman as the future, the much older Frayn as the past. There was a deeply troubling police payoff scandal under way, exposed by the vigorous probing of reporters at *Seattle* magazine and the *Post-Intelligencer*. Some big heads would roll as a result. Uhlman pledged out of the gate he would focus first on hiring a new chief of police to clean things up. His close adviser was Allan Munro, an attorney, and since his boyhood days a member of the Metropolitan Democratic Club. The liberal Democrats now held real political power at City Hall.

Kay Bullitt had spotted promise in that provincial Seattle of 1953. Now, almost 17 years later, the place had much changed. Seattle wasn't just growing. Seattle was growing up.

EMMETT WATSON

Good Morning, Luv

CONFRONTATIONS being the order of the day, we offer a cameo glimpse of the following confrontation: Eight attractive Seattle matrons presented Sen. Scoop Jackson with an end-the-war amendment petition (signed by Bagley Wright, Ned Skinner, Stim Bullitt, Jim Whitaker and Prentice Bloedel, among others). Speaking for the group was petite, but fearless Jeanie Walkinshaw, who told Scoop: "If you continue to support the war in Indochina we can't support you for re-election." Kay Bullitt, another of the matrons, on  Scoop's reaction: "The Senator said to give him the petition but not to threaten HIM. He said we were using McCarthy tactics" — meaning old Joe's, not Gene's? — "then said he knows everybody admires Fulbright's stand on the war, but that Fulbright is no good on civil rights or conservation. He said we were threatening him. But what is the democratic tradition if it isn't bringing your concerns to your representatives?"

Chapter 6

Liberals ascending

The election of Mike Lowry
to the King County Council in 1975
gave the Democrats a majority
that has held ever since.

From her home a few blocks to the north, Jean Walkinshaw would walk uphill to 1125 for informal but serious discussions about war and peace, primarily peace. Several others joined in, and out of these coffee and tea sessions came a plan.

Eight attractive matrons

Kay and her "partners in crime" learned that Sen. Jackson would be at Sea-Tac Airport on May 23, 1970. Why not try to meet up with him, and "Eight attractive matrons" confronted Sen. Jackson with an "end-the-war [in Vietnam] amendment petition," wrote *Seattle Post-Intelligencer* columnist Emmett Watson, on May 31.

It was retail politics, Kay Bullitt-Jean Walkinshaw style. Polite, or matronly, Watson had captured the moment and its spirit.

There is a postscript to this "confrontation." Jean Walkinshaw sent a follow-up letter to Sen. Jackson, June 1. She wrote that in speaking about support or non-support for him in the next election, "I was expressing my own views and do not wish to be interpreted as representing the views of anyone else." Walkinshaw received a letter back from the senator, thanking her for her letter and the airport meeting. The story does not end there.

Some time later, Walkinshaw and Jackson were on the same flight to Washington, D.C. Jean expressed to him the hope that he was not offended by their group having "confronted" him so early in the morning. Jackson responded cordially that he was not offended at all, and added that otherwise he might not have nominated Seattle attorney Donald Voorhees for an appointment to the 9th U.S. Circuit Court of Appeals. This meant something, because Voorhees' wife was one of the "eight attractive matrons" who had stopped him that Sunday morning. As Shakespeare's play had it: "All's well that ends well."

Voluntary desegregation

Education: in a word, that describes Kay Bullitt's primary focus in that new decade. She pursued other interests and agendas. But the challenges and the crises that visited Seattle's and the state's public schools consumed much of her prodigious energy. And why not? Her own children were in the schools.

The size, popularity and effectiveness of her summer Camp for Quality Integrated Education had become a problem. Too big now for even the spacious 1125 Bullitt yard, Kay decided to cancel it. Besides, another project was on her drawing board. In a series

of informal meetings at 1125, or more formally at gatherings in the
Central District or school district offices, Kay and Betty Jane Narver
(at the time a consultant to the UW) organized the Coalition for
Quality Integrated Education (CQIE).

They planned to build community and parental support for the
Seattle School District's voluntary desegregation plan. The Bullitt-
Narver CQIE worked with two other groups, Coalition Concern
and the School Affiliation Service, to promote voluntary integration. On its own, CQIE published *In Touch*, a newspaper focused
on providing information about the city's desegregation activities.
By 1974, it expanded its work to promote voluntary desegregation
in all Seattle public schools.

If even the best-laid plans go awry, voluntary busing suffered
the fate of insufficiency, and in 1978 a mandatory busing-
desegregation plan was enacted by the Seattle School Board. This
angered many parents of school-age children. An anti-busing
initiative won approval at the polls. A legal challenge to the
initiative overturned it as unconstitutional. Mandatory busing
continued in Seattle until 1996.

The result was a dramatic exodus of middle-class families from
the city and its public schools. Seattle's population dipped below
500,000 in 1980, and three and a half decades later, although its
population has rebounded, Seattle remains second only to San
Francisco in having the lowest number of school-aged children per
capita of the 100 largest cities in America. But more than the matter
of integration sparked these moves. Issues with school funding
played an important part.

For Kay Bullitt and her family, these were not abstract matters.
Dorothy and Ben voluntarily attended Meany Junior High and
Garfield High School. It was a time when racial tensions could boil

over. The kids experienced severe harassment. They dealt with this in opposite ways.

Dorothy was "slapped, attacked (by as many as 40 people) and groped." Though some tried to get money from her, Dorothy talked and worked her way around that: "I couldn't have remained at school if I relented," she states. Among other insults she was branded as a "white bitch." These mention only a few torments she endured. But endure them she did, standing up to "this violent, racist treatment" because "I wanted to be there." Her courage, her commitment to civil rights, revealed a toughness of character that "shaped my life."

Dorothy and Ben were not without friends at Garfield. They enjoyed "many good friends who sweetened our experience." Things had calmed down by her junior year, and Dorothy found a boyfriend, Patrick Burr. Recalls Dorothy: "Ours was in many ways a typical high school romance, although dating Patrick inspired anger in some of the black girls who strongly opposed our interracial union."

Looking back, Dorothy notes with some pleasure that "contrary to their image at the time, the Black Panthers were nice and polite to me." A footnote to her point is that the Seattle Panthers' community clinic, Carolyn Downs in the Central District, is the only remaining neighborhood clinic, among several founded by the Black Panthers in U.S. cities in those years, that is still open and operating successfully. Dorothy graduated from Garfield in 1973.

It is important to note that Stim and Kay were not oblivious to the treatment and risks Dorothy confronted. They repeatedly offered to send her to a private school or to transfer her to a safer public school. Her decision to stay at Garfield "was my decision, a matter of principle." She observes that her "commitment to civil rights and the end of segregation was surely shaped by my parents' views."

Ben started high school at Lakeside, his father's alma mater, a first-rate private school in Seattle's north end. It catered to the affluent and boasted an outstanding faculty and, on the whole, an accomplished student body. Sadly, Ben had begun frequenting the drug scene. He left Lakeside and moved to Meany. For high school he went to Garfield. But there, his response to being harassed as a "whitey" was to go along with the wrong crowd. Despite his talent for mathematics (Kay remembers that his teachers said he outperformed the seniors), Ben had to leave Garfield too. He transferred to the Seattle Public Schools' NOVA program and graduated with a general education degree in 1975. With a note of disgust in her voice, Kay remembers that "one of the NOVA teachers told Ben he did not need to go to college." He didn't.

These experiences at Garfield were triggered in some part by the swirling forces of the civil rights movement in the '60s and '70s around the U.S. and in Seattle. Many of the city's black families had come from the bitterly segregated Jim Crow South. Their heritage was one of humiliating and violent put-downs. Stokely Carmichael, firebrand black-power spokesman for the Student Nonviolent Coordinating Committee, had visited Garfield in 1967. He delivered an edgy, stem-winding speech that focused on ethnic-black pride. His targets were largely the Jim Crow conventions and attitudes, which, if not literally in place in Seattle, nevertheless found expression here in more subtle forms. To people of the black experience, his words rang true. Carmichael worked people up and, in turn, he fanned the flames of racial tensions already building to a higher pitch.

Kay did not escape the harassment either. As the co-chair of Meany's PTA, she had a lunch tray knocked from her hands one day while visiting the school. No one got hurt. Yet, while feelings were a bit uneasy at times, Kay persisted. The irony was that Kay's integrated summer camps were harmonious, fun and successful, an idyllic retreat from the tensions beyond the peaceful confines of 1125.

Bumbershoot

Kay's already full plate took on another helping of work. She occasionally invited local artists to the house for small intimate concerts, the yard being a lovely venue in the good-weather months. So when Mayor Wes Uhlman decided to mount an initiative to promote the arts, he invited Kay to be involved. Uhlman had met New York City Mayor John Lindsay, who had sponsored a successful Mayor's Arts Festival in the Big Apple. Lindsay invited Uhlman and San Francisco Mayor Joseph Alioto to visit New York to see how the festival operated. Uhlman returned to Seattle all fired up to start one here.

For his Seattle project, Uhlman put $25,000 in the budget (the Greater Seattle Chamber of Commerce was asked but declined to put up a similar amount) and selected C. David Hughbanks of the Seattle Center staff to organize it. At the time, there was a State Arts Commission and one for King County, but no arts commission as part of city government. Hughbanks pulled together a steering committee that included Kay. The result was the Mayor's Arts Festival of 1971.

Kay found the first couple of festivals good enough but, along with her colleagues, thought it too narrow, being limited to opera and other traditional styles of music, even though it included some country and some rock 'n' roll. The mayor wanted an event that appealed more to younger people. Along with a few veteran supporters of the arts, Hughbanks brought onto the steering committee younger people not necessarily involved in the city's civic life. "We looked at what we had and thought it too exclusionary," Kays recalls of the committee's work. "We wanted something more accessible." Bumbershoot was born. "Well, it always rains on Labor Day weekend, doesn't it?" she asks rhetorically.

While the first two festivals had attracted crowds in the tens of thousands, perhaps 50,000 in '72, the first Bumbershoot event drew 200,000 over a five-day period. While the first two festivals included some out-of-town talent, Bumbershoot brought in major jazz, rock and folk artists. Down to the present day, Bumbershoot remains hugely popular and is one of the important legacies of Wes Uhlman's time as mayor.

Looking back on the work of Hughbanks, Kay and the committee, the former mayor admitted, "I kind of liked the title 'Mayor's Arts Festival.' But, they liked Bumbershoot. They made the right call."

Saving the Market

Uhlman's success with Bumbershoot came after he'd committed a significant error of judgment early in his mayoralty. Among the issues facing the city when he took office was a major urban-renewal plan ardently promoted by the downtown establishment to demolish the 70-some-year-old farmers market at First Avenue and Pike Street. In its place would go new hotels, stores, office buildings and a massive parking garage: 1970s modern in lieu of early-20th-century old-fashioned. Not so fast.

Allied Arts in the late '60s had turned its focus to preserving important buildings. This included support for preserving the Pike

Courtesy of the
Pike Place Market
Preservation &
Development Authority.

Place Farmers Market. Led by UW architecture professor Victor Steinbrueck, who had a key design role in the city's iconic Space Needle, a coalition began to assemble to take on the establishment's plan, which Uhlman supported. "One of the biggest mistakes I ever made," says the former mayor, a slight blush still visible on his face.

Kay and Stim were among the some 60 percent of voters who supported an initiative on the '71 ballot to "Save the Market." The old order, having lost the mayor's election two years earlier, suffered a drubbing from which it never recovered. It was even worse than that. Two new liberal — if Republican — candidates were elected to the City Council: Bruce Chapman and John Miller. Now there was a solid five-vote liberal block to work with a liberal mayor. Moreover, voters had overwhelmingly passed initiatives to cancel an old-guard-planned freeway link running up east Seattle between Broadmoor and Montlake that would have torn up the Washington Park Arboretum. They also canceled a plan to build the Bay Freeway that would have connected Interstate 5 around South Lake Union to the north portal of the Battery Street Tunnel and Aurora Avenue North (State Route 99).

Liberal, progressive sentiment carried the day that November and now sat firmly in the city's driver's seat.

Carroll's comeuppance

Dating back to 1967, *Seattle* magazine and the *Seattle Post-Intelligencer* had opened up a joint investigation into the possibility of police being paid off to look the other way on illegal gambling. Hard-hitting stories revealed this corruption, and in 1969 an assistant police chief was indicted by a federal grand jury, part of the Nixon administration's crackdown on crime. This was the beginning of the end for King County Prosecutor and Republican political kingpin Charles O. Carroll.

Carroll had enjoyed favorable coverage in *The Seattle Times*, being a friend of the paper's political reporter (and former aide to GOP Gov. Arthur Langlie) Ross Cunningham, who had become chief of the *Times'* editorial page. However much Carroll tried to defend himself, he failed to prevent his downfall. "When Carroll learned of a planned article by *Seattle* magazine that would expose the corruption, he threatened a lawsuit. The magazine still demanded his removal," according to HistoryLink.org.

Carroll lost to the younger, progressive Republican Chris Bayley (a second cousin by marriage to Stim) in the 1970 primary election for the prosecutor's office. Bayley went on to win in the November general. According to HistoryLink.org:

> Once in office, Bayley launched his own investigation. In July
> 1971, Carroll and 18 others were indicted for "conspiracy
> against government entities." Carroll's case was thrown out at
> trial, but the damage was done. Carroll left the public scene
> for good. He entered private practice and retired in 1985.

"Enemy" at the picnic

The Wednesday-night picnics at 1125 that July in 1972 were special. Kenan Block remembers them as "ground zero for what was going on."

Of course the buzz among the nearly 200 participants was Watergate, the apartment/office-building complex on the Potomac River in Washington, D.C., where the Democratic National Committee headquarters had been burglarized. Already *Washington Post* reporters Bob Woodward and Carl Bernstein had dug up evidence of a White House connection to the crime. Where it would lead? Would it result in President Nixon's defeat come November? Such topics dominated the chitchat among the picnickers in Kay and Stim's yard.

There also was talk of whether South Dakota Sen. George McGovern, who came to the picnic that evening, would get the Democratic nomination and go on to beat Nixon come fall. He worked the crowd like any good candidate and was warmly received. Yet the senator's star was not the brightest one to shine that evening.

Ever shy, typically standing off to the side, Stim Bullitt attended the picnics but shunned any effort to even approach center stage. Not this time. The event was going strong. People talking and laughing, eating and enjoying shared political points of view. Well into the event, Kenan Block remembers, Stim stepped just outside the sliding doors and onto the patio. At first he just stood there. Then, people noticed him and applause began to build, shouts of cheer rose up, and soon it was a standing, boisterous ovation. As Kay recounts the moment, a broad smile beams across her face: it was Stim triumphant.

The explanation for Stim being a cause célèbre that evening was the news, a few days earlier, that his name had been discovered on Nixon's infamous "enemies list," because of his outspoken broadcast editorials opposing the bombing in Southeast Asia, particularly Nixon's order to bomb Cambodia. This painfully shy man, that one evening, took the applause with demonstrable gratitude. In his memoir, he observed that

> With a relish that might have been malicious if he had not been squalid, I learned of having been put on President Nixon's "enemies list." By degrading American public life and soiling the reputation of the democratic process, Nixon ranked himself high among those in our history who have done the most harm, despite the merit of some of his public measures and policies.

Expanding the portfolio

Word travels fast in "Greater" Seattle. However big it had grown — and was growing — Kay Bullitt's reputation by now was well understood: She could help your cause, particularly if your cause also meshed with hers.

At the Urban League, Kay was asked to chair its education committee, a role she gladly accepted, while she continued her work on the league's open-housing committee. At the same time, Japanese-Americans across the U.S. were marshalling their numbers to seek redress for the World War II damages and indignities (two-thirds impacted were U.S. citizens) they had suffered as a result of their internment at remote camps under President Franklin Roosevelt's Executive Order 9066. Kay readily accepted an invitation to join the board of the Japanese American Citizens' League's (JACL) Seattle chapter. A loyal Democrat and a supporter of Roosevelt's New Deal, Kay nevertheless had been against the internment policy and supported her fellow citizens' move for a redress of their grievances.

Her expanded role at the Urban League and her invited participation with the JACL underscored the fact that ethnic groups in Seattle respected her genuine caring for people who were striving for full, unencumbered membership in American society. In her quiet, unassuming way, never seeking the spotlight or to be head of the table, Kay achieved a status as someone who could make a difference. So, when an invitation arrived to attend an event at 1125, people came. This benefited Mayor Uhlman. In a tough fight for re-election in 1973, against former City Council president Liem Tuai, Kay helped raise money for his campaign by organizing a fundraiser at 1125. The mayor won but later was subjected to a recall drive by Seattle firefighters in a dispute over the city budget. Kay backed Uhlman again. He survived, this time with editorial support from *The Seattle Times*, to serve out his full second term. The election of 1973 further solidified the liberal majority on the City Council. Democrat and attorney Randy Revelle's election gave the liberals six solid votes.

A bank for women

"Joan Hansen wanted to buy a vacuum cleaner at Sears. But first, they wanted her husband's signature on the credit agreement," Kay recalls indignantly, as if the incident had occurred just the day before. "I was concerned about women's problems in getting loans and about redlining of central city residential properties. I knew several instances of people with stable incomes who had been refused loans to buy or repair homes near ours."

The problems women still faced as second-class citizens, second-class persons then, when it came to money in American society, upset many women. Mildred Gorrie decided to tackle the problem. Back in the '60s, her friend Governor Rosellini had agreed with Mildred's assertion that Washington state needed a commission on the status of women. So he named her to set one up, but with no state money to pay for its operations. That didn't stop Mildred.

Early in the 1970s, having engaged her banker husband in a series of conversations, Mildred decided to form a women's savings and loan: a savings and loan of women, by women, for women. To help her do that, she called Jean Walkinshaw, who declined to participate but urged Mildred to involve Kay Bullitt. It was 1973. Indeed, she assembled a selective and interracial group of women, each bringing to the table the character, drive and background that would blend into a talent pool capable of bringing the project to fruition.

In addition to civic-activist Kay ("I'm not sure why they wanted me — I knew nothing about banking"), the original Gorrie team of women included the president of the Washington State Nurses

Association, a Harvard MBA (master of business administration), a real-estate broker, a dairy farmer, the public services manager for Metro, a college professor and an officer of an international construction firm. The group held early-morning meetings, often at the onetime Meany Hotel in the University District. Over the course of three years, they developed a plan and filed the prodigious pile of papers (mostly researched and prepared by Mildred) to win the state's approval. They got it.

Not only had Gorrie done her homework — she did much of the technical research herself — she had assembled a powerhouse team of women whose names carried weight. As they moved through the application process, their individual stature in combination made a big difference.

Now they needed money. Each member of the team made an investment. But bankers in Seattle reacted very differently when approached for some start-up financing. Frances Carr, who with Kay had worked on the Voluntary Instruction Program at Madrona Elementary, remembers that one banker asked, "Do your husbands know what you are doing?" He was no help. But another banker who understood both the changing times and the group that he was dealing with provided help. "Bob Truex at Rainier Bank," Carr says, "gave us the loan to get us started."

Rather than pay large fees to investment banks, the group sold Sound Savings & Loan stock themselves. Investors were limited to a minimum of $650 up to a maximum of $26,000 because, according to Kay, "We wanted a broadly held association with no opportunity for takeover by a small group." Among the early investors was Stanley Kramer, the Oscar-winning Hollywood director (*Guess Who's Coming to Dinner*), who lived in Seattle at the time.

Sound Savings & Loan's founding board of directors, clockwise from left: Frances Carr, Nobie Chan, Kay Bullitt, Michael Hoff, Beverly Smith, Jean VelDyke, Mildred Gorrie, Gene T. Case, Marilyn Ward and Ernesta Barnes.

Photo by *Seattle P-I.*

WOMEN BANKING ON THAT $2 MILLION

heralded the *Seattle Post-Intelligencer's* headline above a page-one story announcing that Sound Savings & Loan would open its doors in early 1977. Mildred had known *P-I* reporter Maribeth Morris and provided her with the details of the plans for Sound S&L. On May 26, they opened the doors. Sound held $1.3 million in invested capital, $650,000 in savings. That was $50,000 short of the $2 million goal. But no one was counting.

By December, Kay recounted her experience with the Sound S&L project in an article written for her alma mater's magazine, the *Radcliffe Quarterly*. She noted that after barely three months in business, Sound had grown its savings deposits to $1.6 million, tripling the number of accounts in that short span of time. "With only four employees, and modest space in a middle-aged building in Seattle's downtown," she wrote, "Sound is unique because it is a woman-oriented S&L organized by eight women and two men."

She ended the article with a personal observation:

> As I consider my new role as a director of a savings and loan I wonder about my changing image: a little more respect from men, instant credibility with activist women's groups, and some rather unusual mail. Some people out there think my thinking has become very conservative. They don't know I joined the industry because I was against redlining.

Seattle banks had been redlining certain neighborhoods (including the Central Area, Capitol Hill, Mount Baker, Queen Anne Hill), meaning they would not provide home loans to people wanting to purchase houses in those areas. A furor developed. The liberal majority on the City Council began to explore both legal actions and means for using public borrowing authority to help people buy homes and/or rehabilitate them in the redlined neighborhoods.

Not only was Sound S&L willing to provide such loans — despite its pip-squeak size — but the Baillargeon family's (Stim's Stimson cousins) Seattle Trust & Savings Bank also made loans in the redlined neighborhoods. Moreover, there were rumblings out of the United States Senate, where Washington's Sen. Magnuson was chairman of the powerful Commerce Committee. His ear was turned toward his liberal Democratic constituents and supporters back home, not the bankers who largely helped finance his opponents at election time. (Magnuson had sent a personal telegram of congratulations to Mildred the day Sound S&L opened.)

The handwriting on the wall delivered a clear set of messages to those in the banking establishment. Eventually, they backed down. Within a few years, homes in those once-redlined neighborhoods were mortgage-qualified and began to double, quadruple and even sextuple in value. Sound S&L not only opened full-fledged banking to women, it served as a change agent for how women were treated and employed at other banks. Redlining eventually would be prohibited by federal law in 1977. But Sound S&L and Seattle Trust accelerated the demise of such short-sighted discrimination in lending practices.

Frances Carr looks back on her experience on Sound's board and observes with well-earned pride that all the original directors stayed on Sound's board until it was bought by "the old Washington Mutual." Sound had achieved more than a profitable record as a business. It established for all to see that women could start a successful financial institution, manage it well and grow it as a gnat among giants. The women at Sound forced the big-boy banks to hire and promote women. By the time the '90s had arrived, however, new federal regulations forced Sound to seek a merger in order to become larger.

In a short history of Sound S&L, Gorrie wrote that this was

The hardest and saddest decision the board had ever made. Merger was the only choice we had. The stockholders would have an opportunity for growth in their stock with a larger S&L. We chose to merge with Washington Mutual Savings & Loan, not only were they in a great growth pattern, but also they were known as a "family bank" and Sound was

known as the "women's" bank so a lot of our ideals matched
somewhat. Lastly, was their offer of a stock exchange not
a cash deal that would have been immediately taxable. The
merger was completed December 31, 1991.

Dennis and Margaret toast each other in Kay's living room.

The "fifth sister"

The schedule of events at 1125 included a first as 1974 drew to a
close. On November 29, Margaret Russell married Dennis Van
Zandt in Kay's living room. Dorothy stood by Margaret as maid of
honor. The reception was an indoor-outdoor affair, which worked
well because it was a nice autumn day.

Margaret, cousin by marriage of Stim's, was a budding mezzo-soprano opera singer. She had grown up just a couple of blocks away on Belmont Avenue East. Schooled in Seattle, she had met Dennis at the University of Washington. They shared a common love of music, singing in particular. Over the years, they would return to 1125 for visits and the July picnics, where Margaret would sing solo and lead the sing-alongs that were a popular feature of those summer evenings.

Margaret and Dennis' wedding set a precedent that others would follow. Not only weddings, but wedding anniversaries, memorial services and other special occasions would make the expanding list of activities held at 1125.

One day, a park

"I couldn't stand the thought of filling it [1125] up with 13 houses (as then zoning laws would allow), Kay states emphatically. So she and Stim decided to deed the property at 1125 to the city of Seattle as a park, upon Kay's death. "Stim liked living with open space. So we thought we'd give it to the city." In 1974, they filed the appropriate legal papers formalizing the gift.

Kay stands in the July sun next to the majestic English elm, Seattle's first Heritage Tree. Gardener Lynn McCaffrey and Zane share the moment.

Margaret Russell

From the time Margaret Russell moved to Seattle with her family in 1960, she was part of the life at 1125. Her mother had married Logan Bullitt, Stim's first cousin, and right away Russell became best friends with Jill and Dorothy. Russell remembers that Kay "took me to a dress shop over on Broadway to buy a dress for mother's wedding. Kay is like a second mother to me."

Russell was always singing, much of the time with her brother Rick. They attended the summer camps at 1125. As a teenager, Russell became a counselor, played guitar and sang as of part of the fun. She graduated from Garfield High School in 1969, and went to England, specifically the Isle of Wight, where she sang with Bob Dylan, who was among a number of musicians there. Margaret had focused on folk music but decided to move to California to try to start a rock 'n' roll group. That did not work out. "Finally, I realized I needed to settle down," she recounts. She enrolled in the nursing program at the University of Washington.

Russell's love of music, particularly singing, trumped nursing. She went to the School of Music, knocked on the office doors of faculty, but only Professor Leon Lishner was in. "I told him I wanted someone to listen to me sing. He said, 'Go sign up for the chorale.' I said no, I want you to hear me sing. He said, 'Go sign up for the chorale.' I said, "I want you to hear me sing." Lishner, a distinguished bass who sang with Seattle Opera, relented.

As Lishner played the piano and Russell sang an aria, he became impressed by her talent. Interrupting her, but with a welcoming smile, he said, "Go sign up for the chorale." Now she was in. Lishner became her mentor. That she was a gifted mezzo-soprano he quickly recognized. So did others when Russell scored high in the top competitions, including the difficult auditions sponsored by the Metropolitan Opera Company of New York, where she was chosen among the top 10 finalists.

Russell moved to Germany, a country where opera is taken very seriously. Some 50 cities have their own full-time opera companies. She won a contract in Essen, and has pursued her career there. In recent years she has been a freelance artist. Among her credits is a tour with the late maestro Leonard Bernstein that took her to sing in London, Berlin and Moscow.

Her favorite roles? Among them are Cinderella in Rossini's *Cinderella*, Rosina in *The Barber of Seville*, Cherubino in Mozart's *The Marriage of Figaro* and Donna Elvira in Mozart's *Don Giovanni*.

Russell and Dennis raised their two children in Essen. Both are grown and work in Germany.

A Democratic bastion

The election of Mike Lowry to the King County Council in 1975 gave the Democrats a majority that has held ever since. It's fair to calculate that Lowry's victory was the equivalent of Democrat Uhlman's capture of Seattle's mayoralty. Back in the '50s, when Kay first came to Seattle, King County government was governed by a three-member commission, often with two of the three commissioners being Democrats. A new county charter, however, established an executive (county mayor) and 13-member council as its legislative authority. Republicans controlled both the executive office and the council until the '75 election.

Yet in 1974 both Seattle and King County were solidly Democratic. The power held by then Prosecutor Carroll and GOP County Chairman Ken Rogstad vanished much as a ship disappears over the horizon — and in this case not to return. In their place were the Democrats, liberal Democrats. To be sure, some

Republicans held local office: John Spellman and later Tim Hill as county executives, with a minority of GOP members on the County Council; and Republicans Paul Kraabel, John Miller, Hill and Bruce Chapman on the City Council. But these were moderate to liberal people, more in the mold of Governor Evans rather than latter-day Tea Party types. As election cycles came and went, Seattle-King County voters would elect more and more Democrats. The suburbs, still largely Republican in the '70s, gradually shifted leftward into the Democrats' column.

The results spoke for themselves. But the acknowledgment that the old guard was history gained belated expression in a 1977 "As I see it" column in the *Argus*, a Seattle weekly newspaper, by publisher Philip Bailey. He wrote: "The last hurrah for the Establishment was the campaign between R. Mort Frayn and Wes Uhlman. ... Since that time Prince Wes has ruled the roost pretty effectively, working out an uneasy peace with the business community."

Bailey was anticipating the mayoral election of 1977. As it turned out, the two finalist contenders for the top job were both liberal Democrats. Attorney Paul Schell, an active leader with Allied Arts and former director of the city's Office of Community Development, and former KING 5 news analyst Charles "Charley" Royer battled it out in a contest that often pitted close friends, and even spouses, against one another. Kay backed Schell. Royer won.

School levies down

Democrats may have become the dominant force in city politics but that did not guarantee every election outcome. Twice voters in Seattle defeated special school tax levies to bolster inadequate funding from the state. This led to the closure of schools and layoffs of teachers and staff. A genuine crisis ensued.

Kay immediately joined the effort to confront the problems. One initiative involved formation of the SSOS Committee, for Seattle's Say on Schools. This grew out of another initiative by the school district to bring together an array of mainline community organizations to plan for the following year's tax levy submittal. Kay served on the SSOS steering committee. "We met with school principals to inform them about their budgets," says Kay. "And we got citizens involved both with their individual schools and at the district level."

Kay also served on the steering committee that was part of the Ad Hoc Crisis Committee, which quickly set up a new organization, Citizens for Fair School Funding (CFSF), led by friends Betty Jane Narver, Diana Gale and Anne C. Hallet. CFSF expanded its scope of activity statewide, establishing a task force that proposed some major changes to the state Legislature. The result was the 1977 Basic Education Act. It drew new limits on the use of special levies by local school districts and, in return, provided increased state funding for schools. The new law expanded the definition of basic education, which Washington's Constitution enumerated as the "paramount" duty of the state. Moreover, it designated children in urban schools as "special needs students."

"We had to work hard to convince the Legislature," Kay recalls. That meant a series of meetings at 1125, numerous phone calls and several trips to the state Capitol in Olympia. When the CFSF closed down in 1979, Kay and Narver established the Citizens Education Center Northwest, to advocate for public schools, promote reform and provide information on school issues.

Moving on

As if there was not already enough going on in Kay's life during the busy mid-'70s, more came her way. "He left," Kay says of Stim. "Then he came back for dinner every night." Margaret, 15 at the time, recalls "Daddy saying 'Your mother is perfect.' I remember Bob Block said: 'Your mother is a saint.' "

"Stim told us in the doorway," his oldest daughter, Ashley, remarks disapprovingly. "Kay was the right person [for him]. She always tried to do the right thing."

Kay and Stim Bullitt were serious people with strong personalities. They cared deeply about their family. They cared deeply about issues in the larger community and world. By now each was an accomplished individual. And, if it seems strange, they cared about one another. Not only did Stim come back for dinner — he said he would not seek a divorce until Margaret graduated from high school — he also came to the Sunday brunches, which had moved from his mother's home to 1125. When they were available, most of the Bullitts attended, and members of their extended family were welcomed too. Kay and Stim simply decided to move on, apart but not estranged, living separately but still connected.

Kay's experience working for racial integration in schools and her credibility with minority communities earned her an appointment, in 1976, to the Washington State Advisory Committee to the U.S. Commission on Civil Rights. She participated in a study of school desegregation in Tacoma, and later served a three-year stint as chair of the state committee. The following year, Kay joined the Rev. Cabell Tennis, dean of St. Mark's Episcopal Cathedral, and a group of Episcopal Church bishops on a trip to Palestine to

Gathered for Ashley's wedding: Margaret, Ben holding Crystal's hand, Kay, Fred, Stim, Dorothy, Jill, Ashley, and Bill Schwartzman; and Melita in front.

promote the rights of Palestinians and to underscore the importance of peace with Israel. Back at 1125, Kay's house was the stage for a two-person play in which a grandfather tells his grandson about the Palestinian experience.

The trip to Palestine produced yet another connection for 1125. Several members of the congregation at St. Mark's had become interested in and involved with the Bedouin Early Education Project, including Kay. There were exchanges with teachers and others working to educate Bedouin children living in the Negev desert. Several of the Negev residents who came to the U.S. stayed at 1125 as Kay's guests.

Local, and not so local, politics

President Jimmy Carter appointed Seattle Congressman Brock Adams as secretary of transportation in 1978. This put Adams' 7th District seat (much of Seattle and the Renton-Kent Valley area) up for grabs. King County Councilman Mike Lowry went after it.

Lowry was not a typical local candidate. He came from eastern Washington, a farm kid and a graduate of Washington State University. He had first met Kay as one in a large audience gathered to talk about desegregation, probably an MDC meeting at 1125. On another occasion, Lowry was at Kay's where Gerry Grinstein, top assistant for Sen. Magnuson, was making a pitch. So when he decided to try for Congress, he asked Kay and Seattle attorney Phil Burton to be co-chairs of his campaign. As a young attorney, Burton, an African-American, had been a protégé of Thurgood Marshall — the first black associate justice on the U.S. Supreme Court — in the early '50s when he worked with Marshall on the groundbreaking *Brown v. Board of Education* case. Well respected in the Seattle–King County Bar, Burton, in combination with Kay, gave Lowry instant credibility with liberals and minorities. He won the election, *The Seattle Times'* endorsement of his opponent notwithstanding.

That same year, Norm Rice won a seat on the Seattle City Council, joining Sam Smith as the second African-American among the nine. He had met Kay when working at the Urban League. Though she was not active in his campaign that year, she readily endorsed his run for office.

PIPE

Partisan politics notwithstanding, Kay launched a nonpartisan project that addressed in combination her primary interests: education and integrated schools, essentially, for her, two sides of the same coin. The headline in *The Seattle Times* of July 5, 1978, read:

Private Help Proposed for Schools

The Times' education reporter Constantine Angelos described it this way:

> Kay Bullitt thinks the time has come for private funds and business and institutional help to be sought for the Seattle Public Schools.
>
> That's why the longtime citizen volunteer in schools here is proposing formation of a nonprofit group called Private Initiatives for Public Education (PIPE) to act as a broker to solicit such aid.
>
> The proposal, being reviewed by the school administration, already has been endorsed by the Chamber of Commerce education committee. It also has been presented to the school district's academic-excellence committee.
>
> "I'm hoping to involve people from the business community and people from the educational and cultural institutions and parent groups," Mrs. Bullitt said.
>
> Dr. David L. Moberly, superintendent, said, "I think it's great that we have this kind of leadership trying to forge a partnership between business and industry and the school system ... the whole community will benefit."

Over the course of the next year, volunteers from businesses, the schools, parents and civic leaders put together the program, which would focus on high schools. In January 1980, several businesses already had formed partnerships: Honeywell with Garfield, King Broadcasting with Nathan Hale, (then) Rainier Bank with Franklin, (then) Pacific Northwest Bell with Cleveland. Kay served on the PIPE board until 1986. The board raised funds and succeeded in establishing and managing a fund that provided grants for special projects by PIPE business-school partners.

Kay had been on the National Committee for Citizens in Education since 1976. Through that connection and in other ways, she had learned of efforts in Boston and Dallas where businesses and major institutions developed successful supporting relationships with the public schools in their respective cities. Her PIPE proposal extended and adapted the same approach in Seattle. It would lead to her involvement in other education activities down the line.

Marion Churchill Muller

"Grammie was always lots of fun when we were little," recalls Dorothy. "She would have interesting things for us to do. She would be involved. We loved visiting her." One reason Dorothy went to law school at Boston University was to be close to her grandmother.

Mrs. Muller died after 93 years of parenting, grandparenting and a career of community involvement. "She was a wonderful role model," says Kay. "She showed us (the three Muller girls) that we could have a family and a career at the same time."

Marion had been a leader, whether as dean of women at
Colorado College, as a founder of the Window Shop restaurant
and store, or as director of the Women's Education and Industrial
Union. She loved to swim and rode horses. She had many friends in
Cambridge, but by the mid-'60s, her daughters all out on their own,
she decided to move down to Cape Cod. "It was a beautiful place,"
Kay observed, "but not too close to most of her friends." Her
mother was not ill, Kay says. She died of old age.

Liberty Ridge

Kay took the call from Ben's girlfriend while back East on Cape Cod
helping to close up her mother's house. If not an omen, the news
was worrisome. It was May, and Stim, son Ben and Eric Sanford Jr.,
the leader, and Michael Loeffler, set out to climb Mount Rainier.
They followed a route that "none of us had done," Stim writes in
his memoir. They reached 12,900 feet, a storm hit and they dug in to
wait it out. A three-day/night struggle to survive ensued.

Eric, Mike and Ben tried to get back down the mountain by a
route different from the one they had taken up. Stim stayed behind,
feeling weaker than his companions. The risk of avalanche due to
new snowfalls was too great. Ben also faltered and was not able
to continue the descent, the snow being so deep it was up to their
armpits. Eric and Mike helped him dig in to a bivouac and then
made it down. Weather hampered helicopter attempts to rescue
the two Bullitts, now separated. Finally, after three days, they were
plucked off the mountain.

Upon his landing down by the Carbon River, Stim recounts that
he felt a mix of relief and worry. Where was Ben? Told that the three
had come down all right, Stim writes he let go a "sob of relief." He

then responded to some questions by the waiting news media and left for home.

In the following paragraph from his memoir, *River Dark and Bright*, he writes:

> After reaching Seattle and helping Ben and Eric settle in adjoining hospital beds for treatment of frostbitten feet (Ben lost parts of his toes), I drove to my apartment, turned up the heat, ate heartily from the refrigerator and went to bed. On the Mountain, alone, I had felt no loneliness. On return, I felt a touch of self-pity for the lack of one with whom to share this recent experience. But awareness of being alive and warm overshadowed this and all else.

For Kay's part,

> "It was a nerve-racking time. Patsy [Collins, Stim's sister] kept me informed by phone but it was three days before I knew they were safe. I didn't think Ben was very well prepared. I thought he did not have the right pair of boots. It was only the week before that Stim said he was divorcing me."

Shrimp aplenty

Few politicians in Seattle-King County's history could work a room like Mike Lowry. Warm, friendly, attentive and easy, with a genuine laugh, the first-term congressman recalls worrying about re-election: "It's going for that second term in the House [of Representatives] that they come after you," he says. So freshman Lowry took no chances in '79 when he contemplated the following year's campaign to retain his 7th District seat.

Volunteers set up for the famous Mike Lowry late-July gatherings that quickly became popular must-attend events— even for national Democratic figures.

"I asked the staff what we should do and they suggested an event. The idea jelled that it should be free, fun and held in the summer," Lowry recalls. "Tim Cottrell picked the last Sunday in July as the date offering the best weather.

"Kay offered her yard. Jim Blumquist suggested we make it a shrimp feed. Rose Kapulzinsky had the equipment. We got coleslaw from Ezell's. Bob Santos and Borvzo volunteered to cook." They had no idea what they were starting — but they liked the way it turned out.

The annual Mike Lowry shrimp feed became a summer institution. The first one in '79 drew 500 people. "The paper said no one would come," Kay recalls with a big grin. "The second year we had 900." For the '80 re-election campaign the Rev. Samuel B. McKinney, pastor of Mount Zion Baptist Church over on East Madison Street, paired with Kay as Lowry's co-chairs. Incumbent Lowry won a second term.

Farewell, old friend

As summer morphed to fall in 1979, John Goldmark's health took a turn for the worse. Since 1973, family friend and political soul mate John Goldmark had suffered from cancer of the lymph nodes. The Goldmarks had moved to Seattle in the mid-'60s. John had fallen from a horse, injured so severely that he had to learn how to walk all over again. In Seattle, he took up the practice of law for the first time since graduating from Harvard Law School. He served as a trial lawyer. HistoryLink.org quotes a lawyer who said Goldmark, "of course, [was] an absolutely brilliant lawyer."

By the fall of '79, friends, colleagues and admirers, recognizing the grave condition of Goldmark's health, wanted to celebrate him. They organized a dinner so that he could participate and receive their respects for his work. The venue was Campion Tower on the campus of Seattle University. A crowd of some 150 attended. The corps of speakers saluting Goldmark included Ken McDonald, longtime MDC member and active in the American Civil Liberties Union — he chaired the local chapter when Kay arrived in 1953 — and State Attorney General Slade Gorton. A Republican moderate but far, in political terms, from Goldmark's liberalism, Gorton praised the honoree for his character and courage. The evening's happy/sad ambience amounted to a liberal celebration. Joel Connelly, a *Seattle Post-Intelligencer* reporter, attended the dinner and noticed an interesting tableau: Seated together at a table near the front were Kay and Stim Bullitt, "holding hands."

John Goldmark died on October 31, 1979. That month the divorce between Kay and Stim Bullitt became final.

With the divorce, Kay's time opened up considerably. Dorothy was at Boston University in law school. Ben was out and about and starting up an antique business. Margaret, having graduated from Lakeside, now was a student at Yale. Kay's schedule allowed for some new ventures and expansion of others.

Benjamin Logan Bullitt, 1957–1981.

Painting by Nana Bagdavadze.

Chapter 7

Progress and loss

Soon the discussions at 1125 congealed
into a plan for a weeklong symposium
that would bring nationally prominent
experts to Seattle to address in particular the
dangers of nuclear war. It would be called
Target Seattle.

The 1980 elections, nationally and at home, brought Republicans
into the White House and the governor's mansion in Olympia.
California Governor Ronald Reagan became president proclaiming
that "government is the problem, not the solution." King County
Executive John Spellman succeeded Gov. Dixy Lee Ray, who had
been a political disaster for the Democrats and was defeated in the
primary. The moderate Spellman handily bested liberal Democrat
State Senator Jim McDermott in the race for the governor's chair.

Although Spellman would serve only one term, most Democrats regarded him as a vast improvement over Ray, whose four years in office were a mess. Her attempts to bring oil tankers into the vulnerable waters of Puget Sound drew the rebuking action of Sen. Magnuson, who secured passage of the Marine Mammal Protection Act that banned large oil supertankers east of Port Angeles near the entrance to the Strait of Juan de Fuca.

The 1980 election also ended Magnuson's extended career that had spanned the terms of six presidents, from Franklin Roosevelt's New Deal to Reagan's "revolution." Republican State Attorney General Slade Gorton took his place. The Democrats' beloved "Maggie" was ill. Gorton presented a robust alternative.

Magnuson, a protégé of the late A. Scott Bullitt and a close friend of Mrs. Bullitt, won election to the U.S. House of Representatives in 1936, then a seat in the U.S. Senate in 1944. He was, head to toe, a New Deal Democrat. Yes, he drank. Few who did could match his performance. He played poker with President Franklin D. Roosevelt. If he won, and accepted the president's check, he never cashed it.

Simply put, it was a down time for the Ds. In fact, many people believed Republicans stood to rebuild their strength, perhaps not so much in Seattle, but in King County and across the state. It would not turn out that way.

Burgled

Meanwhile, Kay had been invited to join the board of the Northwest Chamber Orchestra. Returning home one evening from a board meeting she discovered "someone had burgled the house. The silver was missing," she remembers. Turned out that nearby neighbor

Victor Rosellini's house also had been burgled. Victor was a cousin of former Gov. Al Rosellini and prominent for his popular, upscale Rosellini's 410 restaurant. Kay filed a report with Seattle police. A few days later "they succeeded in locating my silver." A recently released felon had stolen the goods and the police somehow tracked him down. "A detective called and said he would return my silver if I met him in the parking lot," Kay says with a frown of curiosity. "Why didn't he just bring it to the house?"

No parent wants to bury a child

Words cannot convey the draining heartbreak and pain that consumes a parent at the loss of a child. Ben Bullitt's death, under suspicious circumstances, delivered a lasting dose of both to Kay and the entire Bullitt family that November 25, 1981.

What was reported by Seattle news media may not have been what actually happened. Some time before or after midnight, Ben Bullitt leapt from a yacht, the *Pegasus*, about 200 feet off the Leschi marina, into the cold waters of Lake Washington. A strong swimmer, he was said to be fully clothed and was high, on something. He drowned. Or, he was allowed to drown. Or, was he helped to drown? His body was never recovered — despite several days of searching by a private firm, hired by Stim, using a mini-submarine.

Kay took the call while working at her desk. She immediately went down to Leschi, to the *Pegasus*.

"He was murdered," Kay Bullitt states flatly. "A woman, who had been on the boat, at the hospital said they wouldn't let him up." Kay adds more: "Carol Eastman, head of anthropology then at the University [of Washington] said she heard him call for help. She lived right up the hill on [East] Pine [Street]. Chuck Goldmark, who lived over on 36th [Avenue South], said he heard Ben crying for help."

In addition to hearing Ben's cries for help, both Goldmark and Eastman reported hearing a seaplane from the scene down at the lake. Later, the family heard reports that King had arranged for a seaplane to remove Ben's body from Lake Washington. This never was confirmed. But, Ben's body was never found. "His death was planned by Bob King and those people," states Kay. Dorothy and Margaret agree with equal emphasis that Ben "was murdered." Ben's brother Fred Nemo asserts that "Bob King is one of the great liars of his time."

Walter (Ben's godfather) and Jean Walkinshaw wondered who would be calling so late that night. It was Bob King. Ben had drowned. Could they come down to the boat. "It was awful," Jean recalls. "This young woman was hysterical. She kept shouting that they wouldn't let him back on the boat, that 'they kept pushing down on his head.' "

King was later convicted of a different contract murder, plus conspiracy to commit another contract murder and first-degree armed robbery. He went to prison, where he remains today.

The family believes that the seaplane in question retrieved Ben's body and flew off with it for disposal in some remote, never-found location. The mystery remains unsolved. But not forgotten.

Ben Bullitt lived in the fast lane. He used and dealt in drugs. Some of his "friends" likely were not friends at all. A few days before his death, he borrowed $600,000 from five banks despite a bad credit rating. News reports indicate he used part of that money to pay cash for the *Pegasus*, on which he planned to live, and that he paid King a finder's fee of $50,000. Moreover, according to a January 10, 1982, report in *The Seattle Times* by Don Duncan,

> Young Bullitt, of the wealthy and prominent Bullitt family, formed a corporation last summer to deal in land purchases,

sale and management, and listed his grandmother, Dorothy Bullitt, owner of King Broadcasting Company, as a director. She says it was done without her approval or knowledge.

As for the loans, veteran *Times* reporter Duncan quoted Stim as saying, "The irony of the whole thing is that the banks loaned all that money to a young man who couldn't even pay the rent on his apartment and had to move in with his mother."

The police investigation never solved the case. So there was no official closure under the law, no final report that provided the family with all the details of what happened. The impression left by media coverage, principally the newspapers, was that Ben had somehow fled with his pockets full of money. The family does not buy that. To them, Ben died as the result of foul play. For them, the result was final: A son, a brother, a grandson, a friend was gone in such a way they could not even lay him to rest.

"Ben and I chose different paths," Dorothy says with a note of regret and disappointment. "We had fun together as kids, but at times being his sister was a challenge." Kenan Block remembers Ben as "fun to pal around with." About the same age, Block says, "Ben always had a great attitude and a sense of humor." Fred Nemo offers another view.

"Ben's death brought a real sea change in our family," Nemo states. "I've observed that when people lose a loved one, they often take on the character traits of the deceased. He [Ben] wore his emotions on his shirtsleeve. He would throw his arms around you. That was very un-Bullitt-like. We all got over being embarrassed by calling our father 'Daddy' in public. Stim learned to be this gracious host.

"He was a great, great guy," Nemo continues. "He spoke his mind. Ben and I were true brothers. But I overcompensated for the fact that the family had written him off. I saw him freebasing one day in Kay's kitchen. I should have knocked him down and told him to stop that. I didn't. I overcompensated."

Kay is uncharacteristically but understandably somber in talking about Ben: "It's been 32 years now; I can talk about it." Yes, but the pain in her heart is readily apparent. And what has helped continue the hurt are the thoughtless, insensitive comments made by some people in the time since that fateful night before Thanksgiving in November 1981. According to Dorothy, "People would come up to us and say things like 'You must be relieved he's gone.' Or more bluntly, 'Aren't you glad he's dead.' Or, 'You don't really think he's dead? — even 20 years later!' "

With a note of anger, Dorothy comments that "Ben was part of our family. We loved him. Some people just don't get that."

It was a miserable time. But the Bullitts' friends stepped up. Many stopped by, providing Thanksgiving dinner and other food and offers of condolence and of help over the next several days.

Melita White Eagle Bullitt

She turned 7 in 1981, Melita Bullitt. Kay was like a mother to her, and she needed one. In 1974, Fred Nemo's wife, Carol Davis, gave birth to Melita, whose father was of the Sioux Indian Nation. But Carol did not want Melita, so Fred, already raising daughter Crystal, took Melita and raised her too.

Melita's birth certificate listed her only name as "Bullitt." That was good enough for Fred and Kay. Although Fred and his daughters lived in rural Oregon, about 12 miles outside of Drain — south of Eugene — they made it to Seattle, where for Melita it was "very

Daniel Block

Daniel Block never forgot how loving and reassuring it was for Kay to rush over to the Block home to help out when his mother, Dorothy, had died. When asked about Kay for this book, he responded from his home in Perugia, Italy, with an email that contained the following excerpt:

> A cool and damp autumn morning in November of 1981, I was getting ready to go to work when over the radio I heard an announcement that Ben Bullitt who had gone missing was suspected to have drowned in Lake Washington.
>
> I jumped in the car and in a few minutes was at the house. I was the first to arrive. I remember telling Kay she needed to put on some coffee for visitors. She had a drip coffee maker on the counter: "Kay, I think we better get out the big percolator."
>
> I then ran to the store to pick up a few dozen cinnamon rolls and donuts. Within a half hour the house was full of friends.
>
> When someone dies, and the body is not found, it leaves an empty place in your heart and makes the bereavement even more difficult.

special" to visit 1125. "It was really the wilderness," Melita says of their time in Drain. "We had solar panels and limited resources. It was a far cry from living at Kay's." Melita relishes the Christmases with the "20-foot trees that Crystal and I could help decorate from the balcony. She made everything so special. Christmas at Kay's was a very big deal."

Fred, interested in probing into the circumstances around Ben's death, moved to Seattle with his daughters, living for about a year

Melita with her children: from left, Cyrena, Keeshawn and Mercedes.

at 1125, Melita remembers. Kay would take the girls shopping for dresses — "dresses!" exclaims Melita. "We'd lived in the wilderness and never really dressed up. All my manners I learned from Kay," she says gratefully. "She is the most nurturing person I've ever known. She never has treated me any different from anyone else."

Melita's time in Seattle involved all the fun things at 1125, the picnics, the games and "dressing up in Aunt Margaret's ballet costume." After about two years, though, Fred and the girls moved to Portland, where Crystal, interested in dancing, wanted to attend Jefferson High School.

Melita would go to college, but not until she had worked several jobs to support raising three children as a single mom.

Another tribute

The caring impression Kay left on the children of friends extended to others of Daniel Block's generation. Peter and Chuck Goldmark, frequent visitors at 1125 with their parents in the early '80s, made a gift to Kay of a statue that had belonged to their mother, Sally. "My brother and I thought the lovely, peaceful countenance on the face reminded us of Kay and thought she should have that for her yard," says Peter. "We had maintained a close relationship with her. She has been so inspirational in the way she communicates her gentle persuasion about peace. She has been a steadying and reassuring influence on us." The sculpture, by the celebrated artist Lenora Strauss, holds a prominent position on the patio at 1125. The Goldmarks' gift stands on a pedestal next to a tree planted in commemoration of the late Benjamin Logan Bullitt.

Lenora Strauss sculpture, a gift to Kay from Peter and Chuck Goldmark.

Peace and friendship

Kay's abiding interest in promoting peace never really took a backseat, even though other major interests and important family matters demanded her time and attention. Casual and serious discussions that focused on peace continued at 1125. The election of Ronald Reagan as president in 1980, along with his hot-button rhetoric regarding the Soviet Union — as an "evil empire" — elevated peace on many people's radars, in Seattle and well beyond.

The fear of a nuclear holocaust was by no means limited to a few liberal peaceniks, whether in Seattle or Berkeley, or to liberal churchmen like Seattle's Roman Catholic Archbishop Raymond Hunthausen and the Rev. William Cate. Former U.S. Ambassador to the Soviet Union George Kennan, father of the "containment policy" to corral Soviet expansion post-World War II, and McGeorge Bundy, the late President Kennedy's national security adviser, and other respected veterans of the foreign policy/national security community, were vocal in their worries about the MAD state of affairs — war unleashing *mutually assured destruction*. Many people, of high station and low, here and abroad, feared the overheated rhetoric of the Reagan administration could lead to war. The costly military buildup President Reagan pushed through Congress only added to the tensions and concerns about a possible nuclear exchange. To people like Kay, the situation called for, indeed required, citizens to act.

The peace movement in Seattle traced its origins not only to the liberal Democrats' Platform for Peace of the late '50s but also to the work of several others, both in protest of the Vietnam War and out of fear of a nuclear World War III. Anne Stadler recalls the work of Frank Herbert, a writer at the *Seattle Post-Intelligencer*, later to write the hugely successful *Dune* novels, and Dr. Roy Prosterman, a UW geographer who promoted land reform in places like the Philippines and Vietnam. They developed a sophisticated war game in which they played out what a nuclear war would be like, requiring a weekend to complete from start to finish. Groups that

In a Moscow bar discussing King
Broadcasting plans for TV shows, from
left: Anne Stadler, King Screen Productions
producer; Sergei Kvortzov, Soviet co-
producer; Andrei Yakovlev, artist; Barbara
Niemczyk, interpreter; Rob Morrow, Kent
high school teacher; unknown woman.
Photo courtesy of Anne Stadler.

played the game came away with a better if grim understanding of
just how severe a nuclear war would be.

By the late '70s, Anne Stadler was at King Broadcasting in the
post of assistant director of public affairs. "We produced a four-part
series — *Classified Critical — Can We Survive This Century?* —
dealing with the devastation a nuclear exchange would deliver,"
Stadler recalls. KING TV news anchor Jean Enersen hosted the
programs. The shows focused on international security and the
Seattle region's relationship to it, says Stadler. The series earned an
Emmy Award, the television equivalent of an Oscar for best picture.

Jean Walkinshaw recalls the first few meetings at Kay's house, where people gathered to discuss and formulate some plans of action. As these sessions narrowed their focus to doing some studies and promoting citizen diplomacy, Walkinshaw remembers walking home "in my wooden shoes, furious that they weren't going to do something more dramatic, something more radical in the streets."

Soon the discussions at 1125 congealed into a plan for a week-long symposium that would bring nationally prominent experts to Seattle to address in particular the dangers of nuclear war. It would be called Target Seattle. Leading this venture, in addition to Kay, were former Pacific Northwest Bell president Walter Straley; Cornerstone Development Company president (later Seattle mayor) Paul Schell; the president of Washington Physicians for Social Responsibility, Dr. Judith Lipton; the acting dean of continuing education at the University of Washington, Aldon "Don" Bell; and Seattle Mayor Charles Royer.

Target Seattle ran from September 24 to October 2, 1982, and proved to be quite a success. According to HistoryLink.org,

> The event was co-sponsored by about 60 different groups and coordinated by the Metrocenter Branch of the Young Men's Christian Association. It included a series of workshops and lectures by nationally prominent speakers, including pollster Louis Harris; David Brower (1912-2000), founder of Friends of the Earth; Dr. Jonas Salk (1914-1995), developer of the Salk polio vaccine; Dr. John E. Mack (1929-2004), Harvard Medical School psychiatry professor and Pulitzer Prize-winning author; and Richard Lyman, president of the Rockefeller Foundation and former president of Stanford University.

Reporting July 2, 1981, on the announcement for the event, *Seattle Times* reporter Carol Ostrom posed the rhetorical question:

> How did a group of establishment types wind up together in an anti-nuclear war program?
> "I see no alternative … (than) for us so-called respectable corporate types to concern ourselves with this," answered Walter Straley, chairman of the finance and Kingdome event committees. "This is no longer a suspect activity."

Straley's comment gave expression and illumination to the kind of community Seattle had become. Long gone were the days of witch-hunting right-wing Republicans with the standing to dominate the public discourse with fears of communism and over-the-top propaganda.

It may make no sense to label attitudes opposing nuclear war as "liberal," but liberals sponsored and ran Target Seattle. The sessions, de facto, were not feel-good gatherings. As the week progressed, a doorbelling effort sought to gather signatures on a letter to be delivered to people in the Soviet Union. In part it read:

> "Right now Soviet nuclear weapons are aimed at our city. American nuclear weapons are aimed at your city. If there is a nuclear war, all that we value will be destroyed. We do not want to be your target; nor do we want you to be our target."

Kay recalls the meetings at the home of Virginia McDermott when the planning group approved the letter drafted by Kathleen Braden, a geography professor at Seattle Pacific University. The idea was to gather signatures through volunteers who would go door to door, and also encounter people at the entrances to the Kingdome, where the final Target Seattle event would be held. Then a problem popped up. One of the event organizers refused to allow the ushers to solicit signatures. Walter Straley and Virginia McDermott got around this obstacle by recruiting family members, friends and other planning-team members to stand at the entrances asking attendees to sign. By the time Target Seattle concluded, counting the doorbelling effort and people who signed it at the Kingdome event, the letter bore some 42,000 names.

A LETTER TO THE PEOPLE OF THE SOVIET UNION

The people of Seattle and Tashkent are united through the Sister City Program, through the love for our cities, and through the hopes we share for our children's futures. Yet if there is a nuclear war, all that we value would be destroyed. As people who live in the Puget Sound community, we pledge ourselves to work to prevent nuclear war. Nuclear war is an unthinkable horror that must be prevented. Our two nations must work together to create peaceful means of resolving conflicts and take steps to reduce the danger of nuclear war. We are working for these goals in our country and would like to be united with other people as they work for these goals in their countries.

Media reports indicated the Target Seattle finale drew "nearly 20,000" people to the Kingdome that October 2 Saturday night. A number of Hollywood celebrities attended, but a special satisfaction came in the form of a message endorsing the anti-nuclear war stance from President Reagan's daughter Patti Davis. Actress Margot Kidder, who had played Lois Lane in the movie *Superman*, read Davis' message to roars from the crowd.

Thousands call for end to nuclear-arms race

read the banner headline across the top of *The Seattle Times'* front page the next morning. The two lead stories atop the page dealt with the Target event, including a report by one of the *Times'* most senior reporters, Don Duncan. The Duncan article focused on the speech by Archibald Cox, the Harvard law professor and special Watergate prosecutor who had forced former President Richard Nixon to turn over tapes as part of the scandal that led to Nixon's resignation from office. According to Duncan's report, Cox told the crowd:

> "In June, three-quarters of a million Americans gathered in New York City because of their common concern about nuclear war. You are here tonight.
>
> ...
>
> "In August, citizen pressure brought the U.S. House of Representatives within just two votes of passing a resolution for an immediate, bilateral nuclear freeze."

Duncan's report ended with Cox's call for action:

> "The failure of just one person to join, to participate, to do whatever he or she can — your failure or my failure — may mean there is just one too few to win the fight for sanity, and so leave the world on the road to destruction."

In an earlier day, the conservative *Seattle Times* likely would not have given such priority coverage to this type of liberal, anti-establishment cause. But times, and *The Times*, had changed. Two generations had lived under the threat of nuclear war. Seattle had changed, thanks in part to the liberals' dogged pursuit of their ideas and ideals. And newer, younger editors at *The Seattle Times* brought a more moderate outlook to the newspaper's news coverage. Over at the morning *Post-Intelligencer*, Target Seattle had always received strong coverage. There was more to come.

Recognition

The Sunday March 13 *Post-Intelligencer* announced the name of six winners of the prestigious 1983 Jefferson Awards for above and beyond community service. Kay Bullitt rated among the six. In all, 121 people had been nominated by readers of the *P-I*, which, along with the American Institute for Public Service, sponsored the annual recognition program for Washington state.

The *P-I* story highlighting Kay began with

Education in the Seattle area is better because of Katharine Bullitt.

Bullitt, a former grade school teacher from Boston, has volunteered countless hours to work with various school programs. The arts, historic preservation, and the peace movement have also benefitted from her extensive volunteer efforts.

"I like the city and love the community here," said Bullitt, who is known to her friends as Kay. "I enjoy working with people in solving problems. When I hear a good idea, I like to get in there to help make it happen."

According to the website Jefferson Awards.org:

The Jefferson Awards are a prestigious national recognition system honoring community and public service in America. The Jefferson Awards are presented on two levels: national and local. They began in 1972 to create a Nobel Prize for public service. Today, their primary purpose is to serve as a "Call to Action for Volunteers" in local communities.

A panel of distinguished citizens selected the six finalists, who were feted at a crowded Rotary Club luncheon. Kay's fellow winners

Mourning the loss of their son, Ben, Stim and Kay share a moment at the shore of Lake Washington.

are worth noting for their outstanding public service:

> Vera LaPlante, who had established counseling services for people down and out at Skid Road missions
> Dr. Jim Owens, Seattle, who worked with emotionally disturbed and unreceptive children
> Dr. Lester Sauvage, Seattle, a pioneering heart surgeon and director without pay of the Bob Hope International Heart Institute
> Glenn Williams, a convicted felon, who worked to help other prisoners, and founded two agencies to keep families of prisoners together and teens away from a life of crime
> Elynor Nobel Zimmerman, for her untiring work with foster children, including 26 taken into her home over the years

"It was a great honor," Bullitt told a *P-I* reporter. "I was quite undone."

With love, to Russia

Accolades notwithstanding, Kay's peace work continued at full pace. The Target Seattle project had grown out of the Seattle-Tashkent Sister City relationship that former Mayor Uhlman had formed with his Uzbekistan counterpart. In that context, then, the post-symposium activity was to deliver the letters bearing the thousands of signatures to the Soviet Union.

According to a diary she kept, Professor Braden

went to a 7:30 meeting at Kay Bullitt's house about "Target Seattle" Soviet program for next fall—almost 25 people there, incl[uding] Roseanne Royer (wife of Seattle Mayor Charles Royer), who gave me a packet with all her Tashkent contacts.

Braden had studied in the Soviet Union, had extensive knowledge of Soviet politics and culture, and had many friends and acquaintances there. She used these to help set up the trip that would take 31 people, 31 "mail-persons," to deliver the letters personally, Kay Bullitt among them. Also with the group was Craig Justice, a reporter for *The Weekly*, which published his lengthy and well-done report upon his return.

The group decided that Aldon Bell and Virginia McDermott would be the group's leaders. They and only they would speak for the group. Knowledgeable advisers warned the 31 that Soviet KGB agents would try to get people to make statements that could be made to look incriminating or that would discredit their mission. The two-week venture was set for March. They would wind up going to Moscow and Leningrad (now St. Petersburg) and to Tashkent and Samarkand in Uzbekistan.

The departure on March 20 included a going-away party at St. Mark's Cathedral that drew a large crowd of well-wishers. The mayor and City Council members came, as did then-U.S. Sen. Alan Cranston, a California Democrat, who was in Seattle to campaign for president. The group boarded a Finnair jet at 10 p.m. and flew off to the Soviet Union — as it was then.

On the eve of the departure, producer Anne Stadler at KING 5's public affairs department canceled the trip for her crew that had planned to accompany the group to Tashkent. Soviet authorities told her they would have to review all the film shot by the KING 5 TV crew before they could bring it home. Stadler said, "Absolutely not."

The time in Tashkent is worth a word, or two.

Virginia McDermott remembers well their arrival. "We were treated as an official delegation, even though we were not official but, as we had told them repeatedly, just citizens of the United States. It was the middle of the night. Bathed in floodlights, we descended the stairway from the plane to a line of soldiers pointing their Kalashnikov rifles at us. They had two cars and a bus: one car for Don, the other for me. The others in our group were put on the bus."

The first meeting was formal, in keeping with the Soviet belief that the Seattle delegation was official, McDermott remembers. "There were two large rooms: one where Don and I met with a large number of Soviet and Tashkenti officials; a second for minor officials and the rest of our group. They put Don right up front near their leader and one of Tashkent's deputy mayors. I was way down in the middle of the table."

Initially, McDermott recalls, they "told us they would be happy to distribute our letters. We said no, we had promised to deliver them ourselves. There was discussion about this, but they wound up taking us to the market, where we could pass them out." The deputy mayor in the meeting, in full dress uniform, later got McDermott aside and furtively voiced sympathy for the group's visit and peace initiative: "I lost my father and two brothers in the war [World War II]," McDermott recalls the deputy mayor saying, "and I don't want to lose my sons and grandchildren in another."

At the market, the Seattleites passed out their letters and were well received. Some of the Tashkentis took several letters and proceeded to pass them out. Suddenly, the KGB stepped in and tried to halt the distribution. Just as suddenly, "someone intervened, and we continued to pass them out for a while, but then we had to stop," McDermott says. "We had made our point."

On Easter Sunday 1983, the group landed back home at Seattle-Tacoma International Airport. On one level, the trip was a success. The Seattleites passed out the letters to citizens who seemed genuinely to welcome them. On another level, their access was as tightly controlled as they had expected. The Soviets staged their travels nigh like a Hollywood production. They choreographed and observed all the Seattleites' movements, and cut short their attempts to talk freely one-on-one with ordinary people. This was, after all, the Cold War, which was far from over.

By summer, Kay's house was host to another Target Seattle meeting, a committee reunion at 1125 followed by the executive committee discussing next steps for their plan to stage a large number of in-home discussions on attitudes toward the Soviet Union. Those would be held during the fall.

The Seattleites' peace initiatives drew praise and condemnation, depending upon one's point of view and/or political agenda. Perhaps the most significant criticism — was it in effect a compliment? — came in 1988, in a news conference sponsored by the Hearst Newspapers (which included the *P-I*) at their Washington, D.C., news bureau.

The *Post-Intelligencer's* Joel Connelly, at the time its correspondent in the nation's capital, participated with his colleagues from other Hearst papers. Secretary of State George Shultz was the featured newsmaker. Connelly remembers that he gave mostly "stock answers" to the questions he was asked, until one posed by Connelly: "Whether the Seattle peace delegation to Tashkent was good for or hurtful to U.S.-Soviet relations? Shultz lit up," Connelly recalls, and "unleashed a tirade against 'Seattle's foreign policy.'"

"Scoop": RIP

The sudden, unexpected and unwelcome death of Henry M. "Scoop" Jackson shocked everyone. In the short span of three years, Washington state had lost two of the most powerful and effective senators in Congress. A heart attack the evening of September 1 dropped Washington's power in D.C. from the top to the bottom.

Jackson, a staunch Cold Warrior, often drew the ire of liberals. Yet, he also won their votes because he successfully deflected GOP challenges, promoted environmental legislation, ardently supported the Boeing Company and labor, and worked to advance civil rights. He had been the youngest member of Congress when, at 28, he was elected to the U.S. House of Representatives in 1940. Twelve years later he won his seat in the Senate — the same year John Kennedy entered the Senate "club" from Massachusetts. Jackson and

Magnuson were not close, personally. But he and Maggie, with
the support of their superb staffs, teamed up to work tirelessly for
their state.

To replace Jackson, Governor Spellman appointed former Gov.
Dan Evans. Evans would win the election to fill the remainder of
Jackson's U.S. Senate term. However, Evans, a man of executive
temperament, did not take well to the slowness of senatorial politics
or life in Washington, D.C. He chose not to run for re-election
in 1988. It would be 30 years, with the rise of U.S. Senators Patty
Murray and Maria Cantwell, before the Evergreen State regained
the influence and prestige in the Senate attained by "Maggie" and
"Scoop." Unlike Magnuson and Jackson, however, they would have
to work the Senate's corridors of power in a time of deep and bitter
partisan divisions, a level of intense political gridlock rarely faced
by their two veteran predecessors.

When Evans stood to fill out the unexpired term of the late Sen.
Jackson, he faced off against Congressman Lowry. Evans won, but
Lowry retained his seat in the U.S. House as it was an off-year for
elections to federal offices. Kay supported Lowry. Jean Walkinshaw
remembers "Letters for Lowry" sessions at 1125. Ironically, Evans'
victory produced big plaudits for his Democratic opponent. Pundits
and others credited Lowry for his informed and substantive stances
on issues, for building a strong coalition of backers and for running
an effective campaign organization. Kay also served that year as
co-chair of Cheryl Chow's successful campaign for a seat on the
Seattle City Council. Chow's mother, Ruby, a Democrat, had been
a long-standing member of the King County Council. Cheryl now
picked up her family's tradition of activism in the Democratic Party.

In a different place

It was 30 years since Kay Muller had moved to Seattle, deciding that here was a community full of promise, a place where she could settle down. As the city had grown and evolved, so had she.

At home, the children were about their own lives: Margaret back East, attending Yale, and Dorothy, an assistant attorney general, practicing law in Seattle and living with her future husband, Jim Hailey. Ashley and her husband, Dr. Bill Schwartzman, lived in Chicago with their daughter, Emma. Fred had married, then divorced, and as a single dad was raising his two daughters, Melita and Crystal. Jill, an artist, at this time remained single. Even so, 1125 was not so much an empty nest as it was a place for people to visit, to gather for a recital or discussion over one issue or another, or simply to drop in for a chat and a catching up. Kay also made time for occasional trips abroad, often with her close friend from Cambridge, Marge "Muggie" Boetter.

Kay Bullitt kept busy, there being no pause button on the panel of her various activities. For us, however, let's use her Jefferson Award for public service to pause and take stock of all she had going on in 1983 as she approached her 58th birthday.

There were her political activities as discussed, including co-chairing the election campaign committee for Cheryl Chow, who won a seat on the Seattle City Council. There was her work with Target Seattle, and, of course, the July picnics. She also remained active on the boards of the Seattle Opportunities Industrialization Center, Northwest Seaport, the Historic Seattle Preservation & Development Authority and the Northwest Chamber Orchestra. She also remained on the boards of the Bullitt Foundation and Sound Savings & Loan.

Education remained foursquare in her sights, including continued work on the University of Washington Visiting Committee to
the History Department, and on the boards of PIPE, the Citizens
Education Center Northwest, the National Committee for Citizens
in Education and The Evergreen State College Foundation, a new
assignment courtesy of Dan Evans, who at that time served as
president of The Evergreen State College in Olympia.

The state Legislature had passed a bill calling for a review
of all areas of education in Washington. In the follow-up to the
work required, Evans nominated Kay to serve on the Washington
State Temporary Committee on Educational Policies, Structure
and Management. From this main committee, Kay chaired its
Subcommittee on Early Childhood Education. Their work over the
next two years culminated in a formal report to the Legislature,
entitled "The Paramount Duty," delivered in 1985.

A Seattle resident now for 30 years, Kay's roots ran deep and
wide. She'd built a constellation of relationships and become
engaged in a wide variety of activities in the community. Seattle
now stood as the cultural center of a metropolis of 2 million people.
It was the financial capital of the region, where one would go to
raise big dollars for political campaigns, and was a locus of creative
energy, emanating in many directions at once. No longer was it
a burg, the provincial, Republican city she chose to settle in three
decades earlier.

Seattle's theater scene included not only the successful Seattle
Repertory Theatre, but also A Contemporary Theatre (ACT),
Intiman Theatre, plus several respectable smaller theater groups.
Gone were the Aqua Theatre at Green Lake and the Showboat at
the UW. The Opera House was the venue of the Seattle Symphony,

the Seattle Opera and Pacific Northwest Ballet. Gone was the old Orpheum movie palace, giving way to the development of the Westin Hotels' twin ("corncob") towers in its place. The Seattle Symphony had evolved into a well-regarded orchestra that after 1983 would make 125 recordings, travel widely and earn 12 Grammy nominations for its performances under the direction of maestro Gerard Schwarz. Pacific Northwest Ballet had joined the Seattle Symphony Orchestra and Seattle Opera as the "big three" on the city's arts docket. Seattle Opera already had scored success with a summer staging of Wagner's entire *Ring* cycle. The Seattle Center's Northwest Folklife Festival, staged each Memorial Day weekend, and Bumbershoot, on Labor Day weekend, thrived and drew large crowds. There was music aplenty at Meany Hall on the UW campus, with its World Music Series selling out regularly. Each summer Kay's beloved Gilbert and Sullivan Society filled the Seattle Center Playhouse with large and loyal audiences. It was not 1953 anymore, anywhere in Seattle, but the Seafair summer festival lived on with its ever-popular Torchlight Parade and the Navy's Blue Angels flying acrobatic formations over the hydroplane boat races on Lake Washington.

In 1983 there were three national-level professional sports teams: baseball (Mariners), football (Seahawks) and basketball (SuperSonics) — National Basketball Association champions in '79 — propelling the city to what sports fans regarded as big-league status. The restaurant scene had expanded and flourished. Besides top-line Canlis and Rosellini's 410, several hotels added outstanding restaurants. New, very good seafood and steak houses took root. And a growing number of first-rate Asian eateries (including some serving Chinese dim sum and a few Indian spots with tandoor ovens) opened up, as did upscale sports pubs and some outstanding French restaurants. The restored Pike Place Farmers Market, offering fresh food stalls, quirky shops, restaurants, artisans peddling works from day stalls and fishmongers, had become a must-visit stop for tourists and locals alike.

If racial discrimination still existed — and it did, if in more nuanced guises — real estate businesses now made a point of promoting open-housing practices. Ethnic minorities served in elective offices and held senior administrative positions in local government. Seattle's public schools were integrating, thanks to mandatory busing. But many middle-class white families had shifted their children to private or parochial schools. Not a few even decamped for the suburbs and the perceived less-troubled public schools there. The tenor of the city largely embraced the notion that women belonged in a man's world, even though, throughout the city, many glass ceilings remained to be broken. The success of Sound Savings & Loan demonstrated the point.

Academically, the growth and evolution of the University of Washington, in particular its medical school and affiliated research facilities, put Seattle high on the list for cities with an acclaimed, top-tier research university, attracting thousands of well-educated new faculty and staff. The Jesuit-run Seattle University and the Methodist-founded Seattle Pacific University likewise enjoyed respect as good regional midsize schools and reinforced the city's reputation as being the locus for a good college education. The state's community colleges — including three in Seattle by 1983 — were highly regarded, with several offering specialties that led students into specific careers or on pathways to a four-year school.

The medical community in 1983 compared favorably with any other in the United States. Whether it was the University of

Washington's medical school, which fostered the development of the first artificial kidney in 1962; the Fred Hutchinson Cancer Research Center, inaugurated in 1975; a roster of first-rate hospitals; and the success of Group Health Cooperative, that "communist" nonprofit group practice and hospital, Seattle was strong and getting stronger. Sen. Magnuson had successfully steered federal funds to the UW and other medical research activities here. In sum, medical activity from general practice to high-end basic research, serving patients from the entire Northwest and Alaska, was now an important and growing component of the local economy.

Nevertheless, Seattle's economy still rested on the successes or failures of the Boeing Company and the Port of Seattle, which was transitioning into a major facility for container ships. Also continuing were earnest efforts to diversify the economy, with a focus on building relationships to boost international trade. The Greater Seattle Chamber of Commerce, no longer calling the city's shots politically, had adopted many new progressive initiatives and found ways to cooperate with the new leadership at City Hall and at the King County Courthouse. Several business leaders, in fact, were outspoken Democrats — like Target Seattle leader Walter Straley, president of Pacific Northwest Bell.

Even the newspapers had changed. "Fairview Fanny," as the evening *Seattle Times* had been known, was no longer reliably Republican. Hearst's morning *Post-Intelligencer* had become both liberal and a regular — but not always — a supporter of Democrats.

These and other changes could be marked as liberals' victories. Perhaps more valid is a credit for encouraging a more open-minded, outward-looking community. Whoever deserves the credit, Seattle's political and cultural evolution moved in the direction Kay Bullitt

and the liberal Democrats of 1953 had hoped for, had worked for
and had helped to shape. Moreover, they were not finished.

1984 — not the book

The Orwellian, totalitarian view of the world of 1984 did not
visit Washington state, nor other environs in the USA. Instead,
the Democratic Party's ascendance continued and celebrated
the election of Democrat Booth Gardner as Washington state's
governor. The former Pierce County executive ran hard on
education. He built his campaign with many of the late Sen.
Jackson's leading supporters and some of his staff. His reclaiming
of the governor's mansion in Olympia for his party would begin a
string of Democratic gubernatorial victories lasting down to the
present day.

The Lowry shrimp feeds Kay had hosted put 1125 squarely on
the political map. So when former Vice President Walter Mondale,
a popular onetime senator from Minnesota and its Democratic-
Farmer-Labor Party, came to Seattle as a candidate for president,
an event at Kay's was a natural stop to meet, greet and raise money.
Days before his arrival, Secret Service agents descended upon Kay's
house and neighborhood to study how best to provide security for
Mondale's visit.

By summer local campaigns got under way. Kay supported Jesse
Wineberry for the state Legislature and Mike Lowry for another
term in Congress. His shrimp feed that year included a visit by
U.S. Sen. Alan Cranston of California, a pre-convention hopeful
for president. A standard feature of the shrimp feeds was Lowry's
air-thumping, arm-waving speeches. This time, among his topics
was the violence in Central America, particularly in El Salvador
and Nicaragua, and the Reagan administration's policy of support

for its brutal Contra rebels. (Seattle and Managua, Nicaragua, had become sister cities. Kay, sympathetic with Lowry's position on Nicaragua, joined the Seattle-sister city delegation that visited Managua that year.)

Kay again sponsored the July Wednesday-evening picnics, attended in some cases by the third-generation infants of original attendees. As the year turned and President Ronald Reagan was elected to a second term, family matters had picked up at 1125. Dorothy and Jim Hailey became engaged.

Dorothy: "The dress I wore was Aunt Patsy's. It fit perfectly without alteration."

Dorothy's wedding

Dorothy and Jim's wedding took place at 1125 on June 15, 1985. Margaret Russell, back from Germany, sang Handel's "Largo," to the accompaniment of Bonnie Blanchard, one of Seattle's top flutists and flute teachers. It was a gala, happy affair. Lovely weather, a host of family and friends in attendance, the wedding stood out as a highlight of many family events held since the marriage of Russell and Van Zandt 11 years earlier.

July 4th picnics

During the '80s the distinguished Dr. Giovanni Costigan, a brilliant and very popular history professor at the University of Washington, and a liberal of the first water, was a featured speaker at the Central America Peace Campaign's annual Fourth of July picnic at 1125. The erudite Dr. Costigan, in forceful but eloquent terms, denounced U.S. intervention in El Salvador and Nicaragua.

Newspaper listings of Fourth of July events advised readers to: "Bring a blanket; games, beverages and Central American food will be available, 1 to 6 p.m. at Kay Bullitt's house, 1125 E. Harvard St. $5-$10; children free." Proceeds would benefit the Central America Peace Campaign.

The liberal UW history professor Giovanni Costigan addresses Kay's guests at a Fourth of July picnic.

Another tragedy

As 1985 wound down, the Christmas holiday season experienced a tragic shot that pierced Seattle's heart. The Bullitt family tradition called for celebrating on Christmas Eve. There was, however, a gruesome turn to that day.

A madman, having "heard" that Chuck Goldmark, then the attorney for the Washington State Democratic Party, and his family were communists, knocked on the front door of their Madrona neighborhood home, bound them up and killed them. HistoryLink.org sums up the horrible event this way:

> The stranger, David L. Rice, tied up Goldmark, his wife and their two children, 10 and 12, chloroformed them, and beat them to death. Rice later said he said he did it because he had heard a passing reference, during a meeting of an ultra-right-wing organization, that the Goldmark family was communist. Rice regarded himself as a soldier in the war against communism and said that "sometimes soldiers have to kill." … He thought the attack would bring him recognition for striking a blow against Communism.

There was legitimate fear that Chuck Goldmark's brother, Peter, and his family might also be subject to attack. So Kay asked them to come stay at 1125 (without telling anyone where there were) until it was clear they no longer were in harm's way. The Goldmarks stood among Kay's earliest friends in the Pacific Northwest. They had joined in the fun at the Keechelus Conference outings in the mid-'50s. Peter remembers visiting the Bullitts at their new home on Harvard, romping in the big yard, playing with the Bullitt kids. "I remember that home when it was first built," says Peter. "We always had the feeling that we were special guests. Kay is the most welcoming person."

Eventually, Rice was captured, convicted and sent to prison for life. The Peter Goldmarks could then resume their normal lives.

Clearly, Rice was a mental case. And yet, it is not difficult to wonder about the unintended effects that voicing political hatreds can spawn. John and Sally Goldmark had been slandered and tormented in legal and societal terms for their liberalism and partial sympathies with some communist ideas. Somehow these anti-Goldmark antipathies worked their way down to influence David Rice. As a result, Chuck, his wife and their two boys tragically paid the ultimate price.

Another year

At the national level, the conservative forces in America coalesced in the ascendancy of GOP conservative President Ronald Reagan. Liberal Democrats in Washington state who fretted their fortunes might be waning took heart in the 1986 election of Brock Adams to the U.S. Senate. Long a member of the MDC, Adams had represented the 7th District until President Jimmy Carter appointed him secretary of the U.S. Department of Transportation. With Carter's loss to Reagan in 1980, Adams left his federal transportation post and returned to the private practice of law. But he remained in the minds of Democrats hoping to unseat U.S. Sen. Slade Gorton, a Chicago-born Republican with Yankee ancestry, who in the year of the Reagan landslide had triumphed over the aging and ailing Warren G. Magnuson. Over the years, the rather moderate Gorton had moved to the political right to march more in step with the national resurgence of ultra-conservative Republicans. When the votes were counted in Olympia, however, in 1986, Adams won, returning the former Magnuson seat to the Democratic column.

Two years later, Washington voters again sent Gorton to the
U.S. Senate, rejecting the candidacy of Kay's longtime friend Mike
Lowry, who had decided to give up his House seat. The close vote,
however, found Gorton winning by barely more than two percent-
age points. Just as important, Lowry won praise for having run a
standup, issues-oriented campaign, for amassing a solid campaign
organization, for able fundraising and, in sum, for demonstrating
wide voter appeal on both sides of the Cascade Mountains. Post-
election analyses typically included comments that Lowry should be
considered a viable Democratic candidate for governor in '92.

The other major offices on the ballot went to the Democrats.
Voters handily returned Gardner to the governor's office and also
gave the state's 10 presidential electoral votes to Democrat Michael
Dukakis, who lost to Vice President George H.W. Bush.

By no means was activity at 1125 limited to politics. Kay's
support for local artists and typically for smaller groups getting
started brought a wide variety of performers and writers to her
house and yard, sometimes with happy if unplanned consequences.
A flamenco dance group performed there one evening. The
occasion raised money for the Seattle Center. It also occasioned the
meeting of Stim's sister Harriet Bullitt and a young Russian émigré
Alexandre Veronin. "Alexandre is wonderful," says Kay. "We all fell
in love with Alex," says Dorothy. For Harriet, then widowed, and
Alex, the convergence blossomed. Three years later they married
even though he was 35 years her junior. In an interview with *The
Seattle Times*, Harriet stated "He is an excellent partner."

Kay's high standing with Seattle's African-American community
helped presidential candidate Jesse Jackson in the summer of '87.
The Rev. Jackson had encountered some difficulty gaining traction

in Washington state. So the Democratic Party contacted Kay and a fundraiser was held at 1125. Savvy Democrats had come to understand that events at Kay Bullitt's home were not to be missed.

Sisters-in-law

Patsy Collins and Harriet Bullitt at a news conference announcing their gift of classical music radio station KING FM 98.1 to a nonprofit organization.

It is no coincidence that Kay's two sisters-in-law are strong, accomplished women. Society today largely discounts bloodlines, but the Bullitt sisters most certainly inherited strong genes. Each warrants a book of her own. Below is a much too brief glimpse of each.

Patsy Collins

The late Dorothy Priscilla (Patsy) Bullitt Collins was her parents' second child. She grew up in Seattle and went east to attend Vassar College. Home for summer break, she met her true love Larry Norman. She lost him during World War II, when he was on his last bombing run over Germany. Later she married Josiah Collins VI. They raised three sons in San Diego, where they moved to liberate themselves from the too often close oversight of her mother. Before their move, however, Patsy and Kay became close, being young mothers and often together on joint family outings. The Collins family had a Chinese junk that made for fun sailing.

Patsy became chairman of the board of King Broadcasting in 1974. When her grandparents' home on First Hill was threatened with demolition to make way for commercial development, she assured its preservation by buying it and starting a catering business to finance its maintenance. The Stimson-Green Mansion is now a designated Seattle landmark that Patsy donated to the Washington Trust for Historic Preservation shortly before her death.

Another project of Patsy's speaks well to her interests and character. Collins found out that a parking lot adjacent to the Stimson-Green Mansion might fall prey to developers. She bought it, then sold it (at a loss) to the nonprofit Seattle Housing Resources Group for low-income housing. Of the transaction, she told the *Seattle Post-Intelligencer*:

> "Elderly people have to be able to live close to medical centers, on bus lines, near parks and they have to be able to walk to the Bon Marche," she said. "And younger low-income people have to be able to live near where they work, not out in Burien. Wealthy people can choose where they live but the elderly and poor don't have that option."

Collins and her sister, Harriet, eventually donated their radio station Classical KING FM to a nonprofit featuring classical music. It is now a listener-supported organization. The sisters also gave millions of dollars to the Bullitt Foundation that supports education and environmental causes.

Harriet Overton Bullitt

Like her older brother, Stim, Harriet is an outdoors person par excellence. As a kid she loved horseback riding. She earned a degree in natural science from the University of Washington. That led to work doing medical research at the University of Florida involving the venom from rattlesnakes and water moccasins.

Earlier in her life, Harriet married Dr. Bill Brewster. They had two children, Wenda and Scott. Later they divorced. Harriet preferred life in the outdoors, close to nature. Now married to Alex, she lives mostly in the Leavenworth area, pursuing her interests in protecting the natural environment and promoting responsible human uses of it. She founded, with her sister, and ran *Pacific Northwest*

Magazine and Pacific Search Press. She sold these in 1990.
Learning that the land next to the family property in Leavenworth
on Icicle Creek, near the Alpine Lakes Wilderness Area, might
be developed into condominiums, Harriet purchased it and built
Sleeping Lady Resort. She established an endowment, the Icicle
Fund, to support environmental protection and the arts in the
Leavenworth-Wenatchee Valley area. She also helped establish
the Icicle Creek Watershed Council, focused on restoring fish
and wildlife.

Harriet has flown seaplanes and gliders, competed — at age 60!
— in an ironman race, won the New England fencing championship,
scuba dived and served on numerous boards in Washington and
Oregon. In 2004, she received the Audubon Medal, the highest
honor bestowed by the National Audubon Society. That award put
her in the company of President Jimmy Carter, Robert Redford
and the Northwest's own Hazel Wolf.

"She's a marvelous asset to the community and very deserving
of that [Audubon] award," said Bill Taylor, executive director of the
Leavenworth Chamber of Commerce [to *The Seattle Times*]. "She
contributes to the quality of the environment and life in this area."

Harriet serves on the board of directors for the Bullitt
Foundation.

"My mother saved me"

Margaret Bullitt, the youngest of the six Bullitt children, got left
behind, according to both her and Dorothy. As she grew up, there
was a lot going on at 1125. With older, busy siblings and active,
engaged parents, somehow Margaret felt she was the odd man out.
An artist by talent and temperament, Margaret studied ballet and

Graduation day at Yale; rain did NOT dampen
the happiness for Kay, Margaret and Stim.

piano, and took art classes. For preschool, first she attended The
Little School, then elementary school at nearby Lowell, progressing
to Madrona, followed by middle school at Meany. For high school,
Margaret chose Lakeside. She went to Yale, majoring in American
studies, and graduated in 1984. These years included a journalism
internship at the (now-closed) Bellevue *Journal-American*.

Margaret had developed an interest in spirituality. After college,
she moved to New York City to pursue acting and found work
as a page for the National Broadcasting Company (NBC). Later
she worked as a receptionist at Henson Associates, noted for its
Muppets. She also got involved with Direct Centering, a new-age
cult that imposed a strict regimen of living and behavioral practices.
"It was communal housing along the East River in New York,"
Margaret recalls. "The strict vegetarian/juicing diet of the group
appealed to me because I welcomed external control over my eating,

which was often out of control. The lack of protein and sufficient sleep and the near-constant state of adrenaline I felt while there left me off-balance both mentally and physically."

Direct Centering wanted her to take a big job in Florida, where the Direct Centering guru was located. The move held some appeal. Meanwhile, back in Seattle, Kay perceived that matters Margaret were amiss. In conversations with her own sister Margaret, she learned of an exit counselor, or deprogrammer, who had done good work for one of her sister's friends. Kay contacted this fellow. Dorothy was worried too. She remembers her mother saying: "I've already lost one child. I'm *not* going to lose another." Kay remembers that Stim thought an intervention "wouldn't work." She moved ahead, Stim's opinion notwithstanding.

It was Easter weekend. Margaret was spending the holiday in Princeton, New Jersey, with an old friend from Yale. Kay had flown there and was nearby. She called Margaret, asking if they could meet for a visit. Margaret knew then it was a setup.

The event took place in a hotel room and lasted a full week. There was a confrontation. Margaret got in her mother's face, but when a former cult member who also was there mimicked Margaret's behavior toward her mother, Margaret recalls, "I suddenly saw myself and was chastened. I then sat and mostly listened for the rest of the evening. Before the end of the evening, I knew I didn't want to return to the cult."

At week's end, Margaret, Kay and the deprogrammer went to New York, gathered Margaret's things, then flew to Iowa City for a two-week stay at a halfway house for people coming out of cults. This was followed by a family reintegration session in Chicago. Ashley, Fred and Jill all participated, which Margaret appreciated.

"My mother saved me," Margaret says with a soft choke in her voice. She pauses. Her eyes moisten. She adds: "If it weren't for her, I'm not sure what would have happened." Kay was delighted and relieved to have her daughter back. Mission accomplished.

"Mamie"

There were more growing pains for Seattle in 1988. A bus tunnel being dug beneath downtown, as with every other major public works project, drew criticism. News that the project might cause some of the skyscraper foundations under the tunnel route to suffer cracks or other injury only fueled the ire of skeptics. Even so, the tunnel would eventually be completed without any major damage or setbacks. Eventually, light-rail trains would use it. Progress in the form of more sophisticated mass transit belatedly was coming to Seattle.

Progress on another front suffered a setback with the death of Mrs. Bullitt the following year. Dorothy Stimson Bullitt, 97, after a very short illness, died June 27, 1989. She had been a force both within her family and in the economic and social life of her community.

Mrs. Bullitt had not liked Stim's first wife, Carolyn Kizer. She liked Kay. "She was so welcoming," remembers Kay. "She came all the way back for our wedding. I don't think anyone had a more wonderful mother-in-law than her."

After Kay and Stim were married, Mrs. Bullitt "had taken the older three children (by Kizer) every other weekend," Kay recalls. "It had been hard for her when her husband ran for governor. So she wasn't encouraging for Stim to run for office [in 1954]. But at least he wasn't running for statewide office. We lived at her house while our house was being built."

Dorothy S. Bullitt, 1892-1989.
This photo resides prominently
on Kay's desk.

If it is true that the effective exercise of power is in its restraint,
Mrs. Bullitt was a restrained power. Strong, successful, stately,
she used her wits and foresight to expand her family's real estate
empire and to build a journalistic and entertainment powerhouse
in the King Broadcasting Company. And she did it on her own.
Her husband died in 1932. A popular and influential man, he
put Washington's Democratic Party on a solid footing. He was
often gone from home, traveling around the state regularly. His
unsuccessful campaign for governor kept him on the road. Dorothy
dearly loved A. Scott Bullitt. He nevertheless was known to enjoy
the company of others. She never remarried.

A short paragraph on Wikipedia well captures Mrs. Bullitt's
business acumen, determination and strength:

> After Scott's death, Dorothy Bullitt hired a lawyer and
> took personal charge of her family's real estate holdings.
> Her father had bequeathed her a considerable number of

PROGRESS AND LOSS | 183

properties in downtown Seattle, but it was the height of the
Great Depression, and the Bullitt properties were losing
lessees rapidly as businesses failed and their owners moved
out. Working in the almost exclusively male business world,
and despite knowing next to nothing about real estate at the
time of her husband's death, Bullitt personally restored the
family's real estate business to financial health. An increasingly prominent member of Seattle's business community,
Bullitt became a member of a number of corporate boards
and a regent of the University of Washington, and was named
Seattle's First Citizen in 1959.

Mrs. Bullitt expected her children and grandchildren to succeed:
to be serious people, well educated, and to serve the broader
community, but to shun credit for work well done. To everyone else,
she was known as Mrs. Bullitt. Inside the family she was known
as Mamie. As a boy, Fred Nemo chafed under the "Bullitt expecta-
tions." He says he despised his grandmother and did all he could to
avoid being in her company. "But everyone in the family mellowed
after Ben died," he says. "Mamie and I became best of friends."

Mrs. Bullitt's standards permeated the operations at King
Broadcasting. She once told an interviewer that "people should
be told the truth." As a result, King's managers and editors hired
wholesome local entertainers and developed broadcast journalists
who would be expected to strive for the truth. Over the years, they
would win every coveted and prominent award given by institutions
that recognize first-rate news reporting and documentaries.

When a public television station was being planned at the
University of Washington, Mrs. Bullitt donated well-used equipment from KING 5 to help get it on the air. She was a devoted fan
of classical music and established Classical KING FM 98.1, one of

the nation's best classical music stations. The station remains on the air and Internet today as a nonprofit, and is a wonderful and enduring part of the Bullitt legacy.

It was not uncommon for Mrs. Bullitt to be seen, cigarette in hand, chatting casually with staffers in the King Broadcasting Company's coffee shop at the station headquarters (a quirky former furniture store), located on the eastern slope of Queen Anne Hill near what would become the Seattle Center. Her Scotch-and-soda voice was a pleasure to hear. She was a good friend of the Rev. Dr. John Leffler, pastor of the congregation of St. Mark's Cathedral. The two were known to enjoy an occasional drink and smoke together. Mrs. Bullitt, who did not take part in public political activity, welcomed Roman Catholic Archbishop Raymond Hunthausen, a devoted peace activist, to her home. It was during the time the archbishop was openly protesting nuclear weapons outside the Trident nuclear submarine base at Bangor on Hood Canal, refusing to pay income tax as another form of protest and subsequently coming under pressure — thanks to the Reagan administration and local hard-line conservative Catholics — from the Vatican.

Seattle magazine, the high-quality monthly started by her son Stim, one year did an issue featuring women and their roles in the community. One article sought to identify the 10 most influential women in town. Looking back on the piece, there is a strong hint of male authorship. Its title was:

A Gallery of Gals Who Get Things Done

The article included the following sentence: "Although Mrs. A. Scott [Dorothy] Bullitt was named more often than any other

Roman Catholic Archbishop
Raymond Hunthausen as portrayed by
Post-Intelligencer Pulitzer Prize-winning
editorial cartoonist David Horsey.
Courtesy of David Horsey.

individual, she is chairman of the board of King Broadcasting
Company, which published this magazine, and she took herself out
of the running."

It was the right and ethical call to make. Just as likely, though,
Mrs. Bullitt did not want the publicity.

It would be difficult to sum up just how much good Dorothy
Stimson Bullitt did for Seattle, both because she did so much and
because she did not promote herself. She served on the boards
of Children's Hospital and the Seattle Public Library. When A
Contemporary Theatre was strapped financially, its artistic director
Gregory Falls told *The Seattle Times* that Mrs. Bullitt stepped
up with a contribution "that took my breath away." Her Bullitt

Foundation in the '80s regularly dispensed a quarter million dollars annually.

Namesake Dorothy remembers being with Mamie at the funeral for Sen. Warren Magnuson. "Afterward, when we got home, she started having back trouble," Dorothy remembers. "She began to fail, and declared that she was 'ready to die.' During that conversation, she told me she felt 'especially close to Kay,' who 'reminded her of her own mother, Harriet Overton Stimson.'"

Margaret's wedding

Back in Seattle, Margaret worked at *The Seattle Weekly* and re-established her life here. Among the many friends and acquaintances "at Mother's picnics" was the Schmechel family, including their son Andrew. "He was eight years older, but he was always so kind to me," Margaret remembers. When Andrew's father, Don, died, Margaret says, "I felt this compulsive need to be there at his memorial." She saw Andrew again and many old friends and people with whom she had grown up. In conversations with Andrew, he asked her if she would be willing to continue the work his dad had started, doing an oral history project.

Soon Margaret and Andrew were seeing one another. One afternoon at the popular Olympic Music Festival at Quilcene on the Olympic Peninsula, Andrew proposed marriage. Margaret accepted. They were married in a large wedding in St. Mark's Cathedral, three blocks north of 1125. The sun shone benevolently that fine July day in 1989. From St. Marks, Margaret and Andrew, their wedding party and families, and a large gathering of friends all walked in parade back to "Mother's yard" for the reception.

Newlyweds Margaret and Andrew at
St. Mark's Cathedral.

Mayor Norm Rice

As is evident from the many nationally prominent political figures, state and local candidates for political office, other celebrities and a legion of Democratic activists, the annual Lowry shrimp feed was the place to be the last weekend in July. Democrats looking for support, or intending simply to stay in touch with rank-and-file Democratic voters, made sure they stopped by. More than that, the shrimp feeds at 1125 became an important party to attend, as a place to be seen and to restock one's supply of stories for chats around the water cooler or at the local coffee shop during the following week. Newspaper, radio and television reporters who covered politics attended — some just to pick up gossip, others actually to do a story. Besides all that, they were fun.

Friends and fellow Democrats, mayoral candidate Norm Rice and Congressman Mike Lowry share a word at the '89 shrimp feed.

A stop at the 1989 shrimp feed became of critical importance for Norm Rice. He met Kay in 1972 while she was serving on the Urban League board of directors, and he worked as the league's assistant executive director while also attending graduate school at the UW's Daniel J. Evans School of Public Affairs.

When he decided to enter politics, in 1978, Kay endorsed his successful campaign for the City Council. Now he was running for mayor.

Terry Wittman remembers that day. Along with Charles Rolland (who died in 2012), Terry was co-chair of the Rice for Mayor campaign. She says,

> Norman had filed [two days before] on Friday, July 28 and announced that he would abide by the spending limits of $250,000 for the election. That's a total, not $250,000 for the primary and $250,000 for the general. (Imagine trying to do that now!)
>
> In order to do that, he had to receive 500 individual $10 checks — to show that there was support out there. That weekend, thanks to the shrimp feed, we were able to get 300 of those 500 needed.

Wittman, Rolland and Sharon Nickels (Greg Nickels' wife) passed the hat, staffed a table to sign up volunteers and handed out quickly produced "Rice for Mayor" brochures. As Rice looks back on that day and on other 1125 shrimp feeds, he says, "The Lowry shrimp feeds were big for me."

Recently retired as the president and chief executive officer of the Seattle Foundation, Rice recalls that "Kay held a couple of fundraisers for me at her house. We agreed on a lot of the issues."

Rice was in a tough race, but his advocacy to improve Seattle's underfunded public schools, coupled with his support for busing to integrate them, earned him a victory — with about 56 percent of the vote. He immediately proposed an "education summit" that drew heavy citizen participation. The result was a proposed families and education levy that Seattle voters passed to tax themselves to support the school district, such as after-school tutoring through the city-run library system. The popular and successful program remains a centerpiece of Rice's legacy from his two terms as mayor.

Of Kay he adds: "Nothing about her was corporate. She never assumed the role of grande dame. She let the spirit of the event carry the moment — hers is a gathering place — she's been a connector. But she was dogged about the *Wawona*."

Denouement in Berlin

The 1980s proved to be a mix of hard times, with the personal losses of her son, Ben, and her beloved mother-in-law bookending the decade, but with some progress on issues to which Kay Bullitt was dedicated.

On the international front, the fall of the Berlin Wall at the end of '89 produced a marker of progress for world peace. Built in 1961 by East Germany's Soviet puppet Communist government, the wall was meant to stem the flow of East German citizens seeking to escape to West Germany and a freer, better life. Give credit to citizens on both sides for tearing it down. Meanwhile, mass media did its part to build understanding among people, at ground level, below the lofty circles of official diplomacy and the gamesman-ship of national security. Anne Stadler at KING 5, working with her counterparts in Russia, produced 11 broadcasts between '86 and '90. One result, in Seattle, was a sense of connectivity to this historic moment on the other side of the planet.

The Target Seattle project, which drew sniffs of irrelevance from some critics and the angry rebuke of America's then-secretary of state, nevertheless demonstrated the public's concern for peace, fear of a nuclear holocaust and desire for friendship on a personal level. One Soviet apparatchik told Kay in Tashkent that she did not want her family destroyed by another war. These were not lone, isolated sentiments, as the collapse of the Soviet empire demonstrated as the decade drew to a close.

Moreover, there was planning afoot for other ventures for peace that would set another milestone along the road away from the Cold War. It would be in Seattle. The Goodwill Games would open the next decade. Kay Bullitt played a role in organizing this venture too.

Sisters Barney (left) and Margaret (right) join
Kay for her 70th birthday party.

Marion (Barney) Muller Viste died in 2002
the result of a bicycle accident.

Chapter 8

The '90s:
Games and grandchildren

When I came home from giving
birth as a new mom, Kay hired a
full-time, marvelous baby nurse for me
for a whole week in New York City.

— Jill Bullitt

Brunches at Kay's

A Bullitt family tradition conducted by Mrs. Bullitt that Kay
continued was weekly Sunday brunch for family and close friends.
People wanted to be there. It was through her participation that
Ashley grew closer to members of her family. Old friends would
come when they could, like the Schmechels, all the way across Puget
Sound from Poulsbo. Discussions were lively, gossip included, but
typically also about "what's going on in the world at the time,"
Kay says. Is this a liberal Democratic echo chamber? "No," says

Dorothy. "There is a wide variety of opinions and perspectives on all the big subjects: politics, religion and sex."

The Goodwill Games

Planning for Seattle's version of the Goodwill Games began back in the mid-'80s. Television mogul Ted Turner sponsored the idea of Soviet Union athletes competing with U.S.athletes as both a cultural coming-together and an implied rebuke to former President Jimmy Carter's cancellation of American participation in the 1980 Olympic Games. Turner and his wife, Jane Fonda, were both active in the peace movement and vocal opponents of nuclear weapons and war. They brought money and celebrity to the Goodwill Games enterprise. In Seattle, the proposition of the games coming here was the same: build goodwill with peoples of the former Soviet Union, conduct a high-level cultural exchange, leave a legacy of physical improvements and, in sum, advance the cause of peace.

In Seattle, the venture was spearheaded by sports impresario Bob Walsh. Walsh had built an impressive record of turning Seattle into a desirable venue for major athletic events. A tireless worker, he was responsible for organizing the arrival of the National Collegiate Athletic Association's "Final Four" basketball tournament at the Kingdome, among other events. Moreover, he had extensive friendships and contacts in the Republic of Georgia and in Moscow. Importantly, Walsh understood media. His wife, Ruth, a former beauty pageant queen, was a TV anchorwoman at the region's ABC affiliate, Fisher Broadcasting's KOMO TV.

Local business leaders, however, regarded Walsh with suspicion. For one thing, he was not one of them. For another, they viewed him as too focused upon the events themselves, not whether they made a profit or broke even. Some recognized Walsh for his smarts and his eye for pulling off, not so much miracles, but large, organizational challenges. The notion of a Goodwill Games for Seattle, among the business elite who would be asked to chip in and help out, was met with skepticism, in some cases outright scorn. Many of these business leaders underestimated Bob Walsh.

Not Kay Bullitt. Not the Rev. William (Bill) Sullivan, S.J., president of Seattle University. And not Herb Bridge, a prominent Seattle jeweler and recognized leader in the downtown Seattle business community. These were among the small group that liked the idea. "We met any number of times in Kay's living room," Walsh remembers. "She knew so many people. Her work with Target Seattle, her experience in the Soviet Union, brought to our table a cadre of people and a reservoir of support."

With Walsh, Sullivan had attended the first Goodwill Games in Moscow in 1986. Now Sullivan was chairman of the organizing committee for the Seattle project. This was a stroke of genius. Sullivan was well liked and, perhaps more important, widely respected. A superb executive, he had turned the sagging fortunes of Seattle University around — no small feat, given its debts and history of mismanagement prior to his arrival.

To populate the organizing committee, Walsh and Sullivan recruited younger executives, energetic and successful, not yet endowed with membership in Seattle's circles of socio/politico exclusivity. This bypassed the established business leaders. Anyway, many were Republicans who liked neither Democrat Ted Turner's liberal politics nor those of his wife. This would prove risky. Nevertheless, Sullivan sought out the up-and-comers.

Among them was David Sabey, a developer and former Washington Husky football player. He offered to build at cost, to Olympic Games specifications, a new aquatics center for swimming and diving. When the University of Washington was approached, athletic director Mike Lude loved the idea. He thought it could be built above the Nordstrom Athletic Center. UW president William Gerberding and his top (political) aide Jim Collier flat-out rejected it. Fortunately, Weyerhaeuser stepped up, donated land in Federal Way, and Sabey built the aquatic center that, down to the present, hosts such major events as the Olympic Games' swimming trials for the U.S. teams, National Collegiate Athletic Association swimming championships and other such important events. The rejection at the UW not only cost it a state-of-the-art swimming facility, but in years to come, the Husky swimming program would weaken and ultimately be dropped.

Other UW athletic facilities, however, were made available for the games. Husky Stadium received a new track around the perimeter of the playing field and a new floor was installed for basketball and volleyball in Hec Edmundson Pavilion.

The athletic competitions, implied by including "games" in the title, diverted attention from the popular cultural events that composed an important part of the Goodwill program. Priceless art-works from the Hermitage in St. Petersburg, dazzling performances of the Moscow Circus, the staging of *War and Peace* by Seattle Opera, and the world-renowned Bolshoi Ballet stood out on the large menu of choices for those less enthused about sports. By the time they were over, the Goodwill Games Arts Festival was calculated to have earned more than $16 million.

Seattle Times critic Melinda Bargreen succinctly expressed the festival's success this way:

> The prevailing musical image of 1990 has to be the grand
> finale of the opera "War and Peace," the performance

centerpiece of the Goodwill Arts Festival last summer, when the combined American and Soviet cast raised its voices in Prokofiev's hymn to the greatness of the Russian people.

Even thinking about it raises the hairs on the back of an opera lover's neck. Looking around the Opera House, watching many wipe away tears, seeing the crowds surge to their feet and scream and shout during the curtain calls — the electricity was unbelievable.

This was unquestionably the year of the Goodwill Arts Festival — a summer arts extravaganza whose artistic and box-office success eclipsed the more moderate success of the Games themselves. Besides the first-rate musical events, which spanned the traditional repertoire and the world premieres, the festival's legacy of theater, visual art, performance art and dance left powerful memories.

No less important were the kitchen-table people-to-people contacts. Kay hosted Russian citizens at 1125. On a wider scale, estimates ranged from 1,000 to 2,000 people from Russia and former Soviet republics who stayed in Seattle-area homes. And while headlines rang out that fewer-than-expected athletes showed up for the games, and that not as many hotel rooms as expected got filled, Seattleites loved the events. On August 6, 1990, *Seattle Times* reporters Joni Balter and Elouise Schumacher surveyed people and found some interesting reactions:

> "Promoting international relations is always a good thing," said Carol Taylor, a technical writer from northeast Seattle. "It was another opportunity for people from different international communities to get together and find out that people are people no matter where they live."

Archer Gordon, 69, of Tacoma was host to a 30-year-old Soviet trade-school teacher for three days and thoroughly enjoyed the experience. The teacher was one of 1,400 Soviet citizens who took part in Goodwill home stays.

"The big plus was how everybody responded to the Soviet citizens who came and how well the Soviet citizens reacted to the warmth and friendship of the Americans," said Gordon, a retired U.S. Navy officer who operated submarines near the Soviet Union years ago.

Grandchildren!

Upon her return to Seattle, Margaret purchased a small houseboat across the water from her Aunt Harriet on Lake Union in the heart of the city. Once married, Margaret and Andrew also lived on a houseboat there. But the impending birth of Benjamin Schmechel prompted them to move into 1125 for about six months. Now Kay could be a grandmother up close and a helper on a daily basis.

"Ben's birth had been an easy one," Kay says. "So three years later Margaret decided to deliver her next baby here at the house. The night before Conrad came she moved in here. We had two midwives and the plan was for her to deliver in the bathtub." Conrad's arrival proved to be a bit more adventurous. Margaret did not make it into the tub. Instead she delivered Conrad on the floor next to the tub. No problem; mother and baby did just fine.

Another grandchild arrived, and Kay helped out on her arrival as well. But first, there's a back story. Jill Bullitt had become quite a good painter. Kay encouraged Jill in this pursuit, but by 1990, Jill, age 39, was expecting and that year delivered Makaiya. As Jill tells it:

When I came home from giving birth as a new mother, Kay hired a full-time, marvelous baby nurse for me for a whole week in New York City. I didn't have to be terrified when I came home from the hospital alone. The nurse taught me how to bathe the baby. She taught me to nurse when the baby wanted it, even if it hurt. I credit that nurse (and therefore Kay in yet another way) for so much of why my daughter is doing so well now. Kay also helped me buy the significant baby furniture I needed.

Four years later, Jill met David Rigsbee, an English professor and scholar. They married. Makaiya may not have been his biological child, but Rigsbee loved and cared well for her as she grew up. Meantime, Jill's career as an artist blossomed. She earned a Master of Fine Arts degree from the University of North Carolina at Chapel Hill. She and Kay grew closer and closer. Says Jill:

> Kay made a point of coming to my art openings, most of which were across the country from her. My father came to one opening, when I received my Master of Fine Arts from University of North Carolina Chapel Hill, but it was because he believed in attending graduation ceremonies.
>
> My proudest opening was an invitational group exhibition at the American Academy of Arts and Letters in New York City. Kay, Dorothy and Margaret all flew in for it. I will never forget that. Of equal importance in terms of participation, though, was an opening I had at the Francine Seders Gallery in Seattle a year ago [2012], in which Kay (and my three sisters) spent the whole opening standing and talking to everyone who came. Finally getting to show at home was a big deal for me. Then Kay bought a piece from the show and hung it in her front hallway. I think it is called *Anthem*.

Kay's grandchildren cohort did not stop there. Ashley and her husband, Dr. Bill Schwartzman, contributed three, Emma, Walker and Stefan. They lived for many years in Los Angeles. As the distance was but a two-plus-hour flight, Kay took advantage of that to attend Emma's elementary school graduation. The Schwartzmans were in Chicago when Walker was born and Kay flew there to be present for his arrival. Later, they moved to Port Townsend at the north end of Puget Sound. "So we got to see them a lot more," says Kay. For her part, Ashley crafted beautiful ceramics and served as a member of the Jefferson County Planning Commission.

An active venue

By now, the yard at 1125 was well known as a venue for events of all kinds. The beloved Rev. William "Bill" Cate held a book signing for his new work *The One Church in This Place*. A large throng came to celebrate Dr. Cate, who for 20 years had led the Church Council of Greater Seattle. He had championed the cause of Palestinian rights and, as did Roman Catholic Archbishop Hunthausen, he participated in protests at the Trident Nuclear Submarine Base on Hood Canal. Cate also sided with homosexuals in their quest for equal civil rights.

To raise money for the Pike Place Market Foundation, Kay donated a flamenco festival for 100 people, a number the 1125 yard could easily accommodate. The amount of the winning bid was not disclosed, but gossip at the time indicated it was substantial.

A much different event in the yard brought Geraldine Ferraro for a tree-planting ceremony. The former Democratic congresswoman from New York, and first woman vice-presidential running mate with Walter Mondale in 1984, Ferraro planted a plum tree to commemorate the one-year anniversary of the U.S. Senate hearings in which attorney Anita Hill testified that Supreme Court justice nominee Clarence Thomas had sexually harassed her when she served as one of his legal assistants at the U.S. Department of Education and the Equal Employment Opportunity Commission. In the days following her appearance, the administration of President George H.W. Bush conducted a character-assassination campaign against Hill. Liberal Democrats, including Senators Ted Kennedy and Joseph Biden, who sat on the Judiciary Committee reviewing Thomas' nomination, did nothing to defend Hill or to pursue her allegations to ascertain whether they were true. Thomas, a hard-line strict-constructionist ultra-conservative, vehemently denied Hill's accusations and easily won confirmation. Women of all political points of view across the United States were furious.

A bronze plaque at the base of the tree reads:

> **This tree symbolizes a
> tribute to change in the
> ongoing battle of women's
> rights and it salutes
> Anita Hill whose courage
> is an inspiration to us all.**
>
> **1992**
>
> Sponsored by Washington Women for Clinton/Gore
> Tree donated by Magnolia Garden Center
> Plaque donated by Washington Education Association

Not coincidentally, voters that year, "the year of the woman," sent eight female candidates to the U.S. Senate. The group included a "mom in tennis shoes" from Washington state, Democratic state Sen. Patty Murray. Despite admonitions not to challenge him, Murray had decided to challenge Brock Adams in the Democratic primary. A *Seattle Times* investigation had weakened the senator politically, revealing allegations that Adams had drugged and sexually engaged the adult daughter of friends. Rather than face the voters, Adams announced he would not seek re-election. Only then did former 3rd District Democratic Congressman Don Bonker, a conservative, enter the race for Adams' seat. Murray defeated him handily in the primary. Then, in November balloting, she trounced her GOP opponent, former TV newsman and 8th District Congressman Rod Chandler. Ironically, Chandler's seat was then filled by a woman: the late Jennifer Dunn, a Republican.

Dorothy had served as an intern in Adams' Senate office. "Mother asked me if he had ever acted inappropriately with me. I said no," Dorothy states. The revelations ended Adams' political career. Senator Murray, now in her fourth term and a significant power in the upper chamber's Democratic caucus, chairs the Senate Budget Committee.

More heartache

Stepson Fred Nemo (né Scott Bullitt) had married and divorced Carol Davis. An artist and bookseller in Portland, the single dad raised his two daughters, Crystal and Melita. By 1992, Crystal was 22 and making plans to attend The Evergreen State College in Olympia. Apparently, some of the people she met there were not friendly to her. She went to Portland, perhaps to see her father.

The call that came in conveyed horror. Crystal had checked into a motel and set herself afire. Why is unclear. Kay, Dorothy and Margaret rushed to Portland, picking up Prairie Rose Zelano en route, and went to the hospital to be with the gravely injured Crystal. Fred and Melita were there as well. Even though she was raised in Olympia by her mother, Fred considered Prairie Rose a daughter, and Crystal and Melita regarded her as a sister. "We stayed at her bedside those last, few hours," Kay remembers.

There may be no connection at all, but in the news at that time were stories of Buddhist monks immolating themselves as a form of protest. Tragedies like this spark efforts to find explanations, however unsatisfying they may be. Crystal's death cut deeply.

KAL 007

Reduced to a single sentence, the story is about this: "KAL 007 had strayed into Soviet airspace over the Kamchatka Penninsula and Sakhalin Island and was shot down by Soviet interceptors." That is how *Post-Intelligencer* editorial cartoonist and editorial board member David Horsey summed it up. The question was: why?

To try to find a credible answer, 1125 became headquarters for active research into this matter. Credible because, as Horsey wrote for the Sunday *P-I* "Focus" section on August 30, 1992, in an analysis headlined

A conspiracy to cover up the facts?

> The American government could not have done better if it had planned it all. The question being asked nearly a decade later is exactly that: Was it all planned?"

A flashback is necessary to set up what was going on at Kay Bullitt's house and in Seattle in 1992.

August 31, 1983, Korean Airlines 007 carried 269 passengers and crew. They were never found. Was there pilot error? Not likely. He was a veteran and well acquainted with the flight path but had told his wife before this trip that it was dangerous, that he might not return, and to buy more insurance. No bodies or luggage were found. Evidence provided by Tokyo air traffic control demonstrated that KAL 007 was airborne for 45 minutes beyond Sakhalin, over which both the U.S. and Soviet governments claimed the plane had been shot down. The Japanese air traffic evidence meant the flight was downed over the Sea of Japan well to the west, contradicting the claims of the Soviets and U.S. authorities.

There are several other assertions by those who examined this case, assertions that indicate facts that do not square with official versions. There are too many such discrepancies to relate here. But these discrepancies became the focus of work headquartered at Kay's. Eric Swenson and Patrick McGrainer, plus a Dutchman and a Frenchman, set up shop in her office to pull together information, credible experts capable of sorting through facts, and to make plans for a major conference in November at the University of Washington.

There are books, lengthy news articles, magazine pieces, even television documentaries that deal with this event and the issues emanating from it. So why now a conference in Seattle nine years later? Horsey's article clearly explains why the subject merited more scrutiny:

> › Asahi TV of Japan retained an expert to examine electronic analysis of KAL 007's communications. The finding supported the claim that the flight was downed over the Sea of Japan, not Kamchatka and Sakhalin. The TV station never broadcast those findings.

> › The Seattle law firm of Perkins Coie hired a retired air traffic controller whom Horsey describes was "regarded as a leading authority on the analysis of aircraft voice tapes." This expert found those tapes, "which the American Ambassador presented at the U.N. as evidence of Soviet venality. ... which

had been presented as raw and uncut, had, in fact, been edited." As the expert began to report his findings to Perkins Coie, Horsey notes the law firm "aborted" his work.

> A *Seattle Times* investigative reporter, Carlton Smith, prepared a lengthy six-part series on the KAL 007 downing. On the basis of what he found, Smith told Horsey that "a massive cover up has hidden the truth for nine years." Horsey adds, "None of Carlton Smith's articles made it into print and, angered and frustrated, Smith quit his job November 1 ['91] after eight years at the *Times*."

> No less than U.S. Sen. Ted Kennedy called for an investigation, but, as Horsey related, "after a closed-door briefing from CIA officials, Sen. Sam Nunn [then chairman of the powerful Senate Committee on Armed Services] vetoed any inquiry, saying it would be too time-consuming and costly."

So what was going on here? The Soviets claimed the right to shoot down an unauthorized intrusion into their airspace over military installations. They said it was a spy plane. For its part, the Reagan administration, eager to portray the Soviets as commanding an "evil empire," took advantage of the situation to boost its sagging effort to install Pershing missiles in Europe, a threat the Soviets staunchly opposed. President Reagan called the shoot-down "a massacre."

The 1992 conference at the UW produced some new information. Despite earlier denials that they had located KAL 007's "black box" flight recorder, Russia's first president, Boris Yeltsin, turned it over, along with tapes, to the South Korean government. The Russians also released a transcript of the tapes, which, according to *The Daily*, the UW's student newspaper, "has powerfully and almost uniformly supported the theory that the tragedy was the result of a series of errors on the part of both the airliner crew and the Soviet military."

Tom Warner of the *Daily* staff, who covered the all-day conference, reported that Kay said they would prepare letters asking the government to declassify the documents and conduct a new investigation. Warner reported that Swenson

> is most hopeful that the UW itself will take the lead in re-investigating the case. The UW, he noted, would lack the stigma of having lied in the past about KAL 007, which he said "every other government involved in this" has done.

There were no formal follow-up investigations, to Kay's continuing dissatisfaction. Murray Sayle, a writer whose article on the subject in *The New Yorker* appeared December 13, 1993, propounded the view that unintended errors led to the KAL 007 disaster. In response, one of the experts who questioned the official versions of this event, Michael Brun, refuted Sayle's article in a detailed 10-page letter to *New Yorker* editor Tina Brown.

Brun, a former pilot and airline CEO, ended his letter with a most intriguing point. He noted that there were two airplanes that intruded into Soviet airspace that night. He notes that both were shot down. He says the Soviet fighter pilot

> made two sorties that night and shot down two different intruders. The events that night over Sakhalin involved a lot more than the innocent trespassing of a lost civilian airliner. It brought us frighteningly close to World War III.

To date, no serious follow-up investigations have occurred. Kay remains convinced that all the facts, all the true facts, are yet to be told.

A far more satisfying result that same November came in the election for Washington's governor. Mike Lowry defeated former conservative Republican state Attorney General Ken Eikenberry, sending the arm-waving liberal from Renton to Olympia. This time the liberal Democrats had one of their own in the governor's mansion. They had liked popular Booth Gardner. But they loved Lowry.

More citizen diplomacy

The following June, Kay participated in another venture of citizen diplomacy. The Rev. Donovan Cook of the University Baptist Church, located near the UW campus, organized a small group to visit Haiti, Kay included. The purpose of the trip was to check into reports of human rights abuses, the ouster of reform-minded President Jean-Bertrand Aristide, a former Roman Catholic priest, and a threat from the United Nations to "impose a worldwide blockade of oil shipments" on the impoverished country. According to *The Seattle Times*, these all added up to trouble in this poorest among poor nations. Upon their return, Kay told *The Times* she and her colleagues found virtually no rule of law: "The constitution has virtually been ignored."

Kay's Independence Day picnic in '94 featured Claudette Werleigh, whom *The Seattle Times* described as "an ardent Catholic, a member of the Haitian privileged class and of the government of Jean-Bertrand Aristide, Haiti's president-in-exile." To the gathering on the grounds at 1125, *The Times* reported,

> Werleigh talked about the events that have led Aristide to the brink of returning home to the country he was driven from by the Haitian military almost two years ago. Aristide yesterday signed an agreement with his military rivals that would enable him to return to power.

Another event at 1125 that summer was the Arab Festival on August 28. Music, dancing, Arab fashions including traditional costumes, and Middle Eastern food comprised the all-day, no-charge event. "People have a stereotype about the Arabs and we wanted to show them the rich culture we have," Afifi Durr, who is from Lebanon, told a *Seattle Times* reporter. "Many people don't even know about the culture of the Middle East. We want to bridge the gap between the Middle East and the West."

That fall, Kay sponsored a fundraiser for Attorney General Christine Gregoire. Gregoire and Dorothy had become colleagues and friends when as lawyers they both worked on the state attorney general's staff. Gregoire later served as head of the State Department of Ecology under Governor Gardner. Now she was running for a second term as attorney general. Kay made the pitch for contributions that day, an act that underscored her support for Gregoire. Many among the large gathering openly speculated that after serving as Washington's leading attorney, Gregoire would become governor. They would have to wait.

A celebration

The *Seattle Times* columnist Jean Godden said it best. No point in trying to better it. Her column of Wednesday, February 22, 1995, carried the headline:

KUDOS FOR KAY, AND A FOUNTAIN

Last night was full of surprises for Seattleite Kay Bullitt, who is to local causes what the chip is to the computer. Name a worthy cause, and Bullitt is there.

It was testimonial time last night, the day before Bullitt's 70th birthday. About 500 guests — family, friends and longtime allies — attended a sit-down birthday dinner at

Seattle University's Campion Hall organized by a group that included her daughters, Margaret and Dorothy Bullitt, and SU's Rebecca Slivka.

Paying tribute were Gov. Mike Lowry, who addressed Kay Bullitt 's civic accomplishments; Dr. Hubert Locke, her work on behalf of peace; David Hughbanks, her historic preservation activism; and the Rev. Sam McKinney, her efforts in civil rights and education.

Among the surprise gifts: a portrait by Nana Bagdavadze of Kay Bullitt's late son, Ben Bullitt, three leather-bound volumes of personal memories and enough donations to commission a fountain by Gerard Tsutakawa.

The fountain will be installed in the yard at Kay Bullitt's Capitol Hill home, a gathering ground for fomenting many a local revolution.

Dorothy, who served as master of ceremonies for the party, and Margaret had commissioned Bagdavadze's portrait of Ben as their gift to Kay. Margaret added a short film to commemorate Kay's 70th birthday by assembling 45 photos into a retrospective of highlights from her mother's long, active and caring life.

Standing at the edge of Kay's patio, the Gerard Tsutakawa fountain provides a refreshing ambience as its waters tinkle softly along their short course.

Nana Bagdavadze

A native of the Republic of Georgia, Nana Bagdavadze came to the United States in 1988 as a bone-marrow donor. Her sister Zizi suffered from leukemia and was undergoing treatment at Seattle's Fred Hutchinson Cancer Research Center. Her trip here on her sister's behalf had been arranged by Goodwill Games promoter Bob Walsh.

A budding talent, Nana trained in classical painting in Georgia and studied at the prestigious Hermitage in St. Petersburg, Russia. Through a mutual friend, Carmen Matthews, who had known Kay at Radcliffe, Nana was introduced to Kay, who immediately took her in. "It was about Christmastime, 1990," Nana recalls. And in addition to living at 1125, "Kay let me use her wonderful space in the basement for a studio. I got a green card, based on artistic merit. I taught classes here. She is my second mom!"

Nana's painting of Ben, head and shoulders with a white bird perched on his left shoulder, hangs prominently above 1125's stairway landing to the basement. This striking portrait is fully visible as one enters Kay's front door. Margaret and Dorothy presented it to Kay at the large gathering celebrating her 70th birthday. Nana did the work, having listened carefully to recollections of Ben and from observing pictures. "I felt his presence," she remembers, with a tone of conviction as though it were yesterday.

Nana's visit to Seattle succeeded even more than she might have hoped. Her sister beat cancer and today lives in the independent Republic of Georgia. Nana met and married Aleksandre Taktaishgvili in October 2003, in the yard at 1125. He is a research scientist at NASA. They live in Washington, D.C.

Nana Bagdavadze puts
the finishing touches on
one of her paintings.

Nana returns to Seattle often. She continues to use Kay's base-ment both as a studio for her own work and for conducting classes.

Pine Street

The fate of downtown Seattle stood out as one of the major chal-lenges confronting the city and the administration of Mayor Norm Rice. This was not, as some tried to portray it, a clash of downtown business interests versus "the people." No, the issues stood at the heart of what Washington state's large urban core would be: a strong, attractive place to work, shop and enjoy. Or, would it sink into decay? At the time, there were empty storefronts, more crime than people would tolerate, more indications that its retail attrac-tions would move to the suburbs.

Of particular concern was a pending decision by the Nordstrom family about where they would build a new headquarters for their nationally successful and expanding company. Would the retailer choose Bellevue and its successful Bellevue Square? Would the headquarters stay downtown and, if so, what would be done there? A sticky problem was the deal that had been cut by former Mayor

Charles Royer to close Pine Street back in the '80s as part of the project to develop Westlake Park and Westlake Center, a high-rise retail-office building immediately west of the former Frederick & Nelson department store. Downtown businesses large and small, the Metro bus system, the police and fire departments, and residents who preferred unclogged downtown traffic patterns never really liked the Pine Street closure.

Moreover, Seattle's venerable Frederick & Nelson building, now empty, stood at risk. It had been bought by a British retailer that failed to run a successful department store business there. Local developer David Sabey purchased the property and did his best to resurrect the department store. That did not succeed, however, and again the building was on the market. What would happen to this lovely full-block edifice in the very heart of Seattle's retail core?

A plan emerged, but with conditions. The Nordstroms would buy the Frederick's building from Sabey and renovate it into their flagship store. Other developers would buy the block across Sixth Avenue to the east and redevelop it into a major shopping center with a large underground but public parking garage, if, as part of the deal, the city would reopen Pine Street. Mayor Norm Rice liked the proposal. He was willing to invest his considerable political capital into supporting it. The opposition tried to make the case that this was an attack on the people's downtown park and gathering place for rallies and celebrations. The question of Pine Street's closure went up for a public vote. Kay Bullitt entered the fray.

In an op-ed piece she co-authored with City Council member Jan Drago and union official Ron Judd that appeared in the pages of the March 5, 1995, edition of *The Seattle Times*, the trio held forth in support of reopening Pine:

By approving Seattle Referendum #1 on March 14, we can reverse the recent decline in our downtown. With voter approval, Nordstrom will spend $100 million to restore the historic F&N building and create a spectacular new flagship store and international headquarters. And with voter approval, the rundown parking garage block will be redeveloped into an exciting new shopping and entertainment center, with twice as much parking to make it easier and more convenient to shop downtown.

This project is vital to the future of our city.

Both the *Seattle P-I* and *The Times* endorsed approval of Referendum 1. Seattle voters agreed, overwhelmingly. Sixty-one percent approved the call to reopen Pine Street, a landslide by any measure. The vote, and subsequent successful redevelopment, drew national media attention and praise. The Nordstroms would wind up almost doubling their investment in renovating the Frederick's building, which to this day is a must-visit stop for locals and tourists alike. The revitalization of downtown Seattle would stand as one among the several successful initiatives of the Rice years at City Hall.

Lowry's last hurrah

For a finale it turned out to be some finale: A former staff member had accused Gov. Mike Lowry of unwanted advances. Lowry denied the accusations but wound up paying a financial settlement to conclude the matter. Many believed he should have fought the allegations. His loyal supporters stood resolutely by him, but the governor knew his time to step away from politics had come.

As a testimonial to his years of public service, the last Lowry shrimp feed that July was as good as any. Some 900 people came. They each paid $30 for the privilege, raising about $27,000 that he could use to help cover the cost of the legal settlement. The occasion may not have been the go-get-'em celebration it would have been if Lowry had run for a second term. Still, it provided a boost in morale from his faithful friends.

PeaceTrees Vietnam

U.S. Army helicopter pilot 1st Lt. Daniel Cheney lost his life near Di An in Vietnam's Quang Tri province on January 6, 1969. He was like so many other promising young men taken from their families, thought his sister Jerilyn Brusseau. She grieved over his death but determined that some day she would find a way to try to heal this loss. She knew it wasn't only Americans being killed there, only U.S. families losing brothers, sons and fathers. The Vietnamese also suffered the same losses and hurt. Twenty-six years later Brusseau made her move.

It was November, 1995, when the United States and Vietnam announced they had established normal relations. Brusseau called

1st Lt. Daniel Cheney, U.S. Army helicopter pilot. Killed in action January 6, 1969, near Di An, Vietnam.

Courtesy of Jerilyn Brusseau.

some friends and asked them over to consider her idea: organize an effort involving both Americans and Vietnamese to clear the minefields and plant trees of hope in Quang Tri province, Vietnam. "I thought we should reach out in a way that restored honor and dignity, to build a bridge," she says. "They liked the idea." They liked it so much that Jerilyn's husband, Danaan, that same night took a red-eye flight to Washington, D.C., to attend (without an invitation) an open house by the Vietnamese chargé d'affaires.

Quang Tri province in central Vietnam suffered more bombing and battles than any other local area in the Vietnam War theater: "It was devastated," Brusseau says. "More ordnance was dropped on Quang Tri, which is about the size of King County, than all that we dropped during World War II. Before the war, there were 1,100 villages in Quang Tri. Today, there are three."

Danaan met the chargé d'affaires. who invited him in, listened to the idea and promised to help. Things moved fast. "Six weeks later we were in Hanoi. We were met by a Vietnamese veteran and a U.S. veteran living there. The next day we met with Vu Xuan Hong of the Vietnam Union of Friendship organization, which was a nongovernmental organization. The meetings went well," Brusseau says. "The Vietnamese were enthused about the ideas we presented. We were there four weeks. We went to one of the three villages that survived the war. What we saw was tragic."

Back home, Brusseau immediately called Kay. They had met during one of the citizen-diplomacy trips to the Soviet Union. "Kay is a visionary and knows how to make things happen," Brusseau says. "The first meeting in early 1996 to organize PeaceTrees Vietnam took place in her living room. And there were many others there after that one."

What came out of the meetings at 1125 was a plan to raise $220,000, to recruit ordnance disposal experts and to develop the details for the first on-the-ground program. "We had no trouble recruiting the talent and people we needed," Brusseau says. "By November of that year, we had cleared 18 acres of land mines and unexploded bombs, planted 2,500 indigenous trees, and our 42 volunteers included people from seven countries."

PeaceTrees Vietnam succeeded and has (pun intended) grown apace. It remains an active citizen-diplomacy venture today.

Politics and publishing

Kay worked as treasurer for Mayor Norm Rice's unsuccessful campaign to win the 1996 Democratic nomination for governor. With incumbent Mike Lowry out of the picture, Rice and King County Executive Gary Locke led the Democratic field in the primary. Locke won by a respectable margin and easily captured the governor's office, defeating state Sen. Ellen Craswell, a staunch, proud fundamentalist Christian. Her positions proved to be too far out of step with Washington voters, especially women voters.

Meanwhile, another Bullitt hit the bookstores with a well-received volume. Dorothy's *Filling the Void: Six Steps from Loss to Fulfillment* offers a six-step pathway for dealing successfully with a crisis. The work earned critical acclaim from psychologists, members of the clergy and readers — the latter rating it five out of five stars. Amazon.com offers this summary:

> Bullitt wrote this book when she couldn't find the guide
> she needed to lead her out of her crises. It is told through
> the gripping personal stories of those she has known and

A status report

By the end of 2011, the PeaceTrees Vietnam Explosive Ordnance Disposal teams had located, removed, and destroyed 63,343 pieces of unexploded ordnance. It had cleared 216 hectares (534 acres) of contaminated land. PeaceTrees had provided mine risk education to more than 72,750 children and adults. It has provided survivor assistance to more than 783 UXO victims and family members. And on safely cleared land, PeaceTrees and its volunteers have planted more than 41,927 indigenous trees, built 100 homes, five kindergartens, and 11 libraries. Finally, 585 citizen diplomats have traveled with PeaceTrees to Vietnam to continue our efforts to build bridges of friendship and peace with the Vietnamese people.

— from the 2011 Annual Report
PeaceTrees Vietnam
www.peacetreesvietnam.org

counseled, who have found their way out of despair by following the six-step plan described here. The dynamic program is for those mourning the loss of a loved one, a marriage, a job, property, money and more.

The year ended as Kay and a large assemblage of family and friends bid a final farewell to Eleanor Siegl. The Siegl family had been old friends dating back to the '50s. Kay and Stim had helped Eleanor start the highly successful Little School. The obituary published by *The Seattle Times* quoted Kay: "Mrs. Siegl was one of the best things to happen to Seattle and education. There were so few programs for small children and so few places for them to go," Bullitt said. "But she was wonderfully persistent." Two weeks later, her violinist husband Henry followed her in death.

The Little School's success is a credit to its founders but most especially to the foresight, intelligence and dedication of Eleanor Siegl. That it flourishes today, 54 years later, is testimony enough.

Staying the course

The local elections in 1997 reaffirmed the Democrats' hold on city and county politics. Paul Schell, a liberal developer, won the mayor's office handily over self-styled "people's choice" candidate Charlie Chong. Ron Sims became the first African-American to win election as King County executive. A protégé of long-standing state Sen. George Fleming, Sims earned a reputation for effective, progressive politics, both in the state Legislature and as a member of the King County Council. Seattle voters that year also approved a proposal to build a monorail system throughout the city.

Only Sims proved to be a success as the years passed by. Schell suffered from a surprising failure of common sense. His police live-and-let-live response to violent and destructive riots downtown during the major World Trade Organization conference, his "home in bed" absence during a Fat Tuesday riot in Pioneer Square that cost the life of a young, peaceful bystander, his expenditure of $50,000 for a tree that he liked stood out among a litany of missteps that rendered him a one-term mayor. The monorail project came a cropper due to poor planning, hopelessly high cost estimates and a kind of tin-ear political management that proved unable to successfully overcome elementary questions about why and how the project would cost so much.

A large assemblage gathers in Kay's yard to commemorate 50 years of her Wednesday-evening July picnics.

Chapter 9

New millennium,
same issues

In July 2002, we held a one-week
day camp in Kay's spacious yard.
It was thrilling to see the number
who joined us as counselors,
project leaders and volunteers.

— Susan Davis

First citizens

The arrival of the new millennium did not bring global chaos (the
Y2K problem, aka the "millennium bug") as many had worried
would happen: that binary computer programs might suffer a
"stroke" with the changing of the date and minute come zero hour
at midnight, when the 20th century gave way to the 21st. But the
worry and the warning prompted massive investments in high-tech
equipment upgrades. The age of the Internet was here. And Seattle
was in the thick of it. Microsoft already was a behemoth and still

growing. Amazon was revolutionizing retail marketing and selling and would grow exponentially. Biotech research took root and expanded. These companies and many others like magnets attracted a younger generation to the area. If anything, this younger cohort was as progressive, if not more so, as Kay's generation who'd moved in after World War II.

For Kay and her family, the new millennium brought a special distinction. The First Citizen Award of 2000, sponsored annually by the Seattle-King County Association of Realtors, selected five of the Bullitts for their public service. Stim, Patsy Bullitt Collins, Harriet, Kay and daughter Dorothy jointly were celebrated at a well-attended luncheon. Of the award to the family, former Mayor Norm Rice told the *Puget Sound Business Journal:*

> "The sense of fairness, equality and equity in our region is something they stood for," he said. "They are an extraordinary family, and what makes them great is the sum of each of their characters, rather than any one. Everybody's been talking about Seattle's soul lately," he added. "Without the Bullitt family, Seattle would be soulless."

First Citizens: Stim Bullitt, Patsy Collins, Kay, Dorothy and Harriet Bullitt. Courtesy of HistoryLink.org.

Kay and Stim had been divorced for almost 19 years now but their separation had not riven the family. Kay still welcomed Stim to the family's Sunday brunches at 1125. In other cases, as with the First Citizen Award, they would appear together in a most cordial way. This example influenced their children. Both Margaret and Dorothy divorced early in the new millennium. But these partings, while no cause for celebration, did not produce debilitating acrimony. Margaret and sons Ben and Conrad moved in with Kay at 1125 and would stay for about six months. Margaret supported herself and two sons working as a real estate agent. Throughout, Kay was a rock of stability and support. Her spirit of kindness and generosity prevailed; her love and genuine caring provided security not only for family but for friends and others as well. People who know Kay uniformly testify to this.

Another friend falls

One of those very close friends and compatriots, Betty Jane Narver, died December 9, the result of a stroke. She had been a force for good on many fronts, using her position as a fellow at the Evans School of Public Affairs at the University of Washington to bring people together across a spectrum of issues: school funding, environmental protection, health care and libraries. Asked for a comment by *The Seattle Times*, Kay said, "She was very involved with public-school funding, as well as integration and equity issues from the '60s on. And she was a wonderful friend. She gave so much. She lived seven lives."

Being close to Betty Jane generated another friendship. At gatherings both at Narver's home and at 1125, Kay and Julio Ramirez became good friends. Julio suffered from a severe case of Crohn's disease. This debilitating affliction of the digestive tract drains people of their strength, both physical and emotional. In Ramirez's case, he managed with medical attention for about four years but by 2005 required a series of surgeries. Finally, Ramirez faced an arduous nine-hour surgery to reconstruct his digestive tract. Throughout this period, Ramirez remembers that "Kay made sure to find the time to visit me as often as possible regardless of her busy schedule." Ramirez continues:

> I will never forget what could have been my very last view: Kay sitting quietly on a chair next to the bed's footboard in the middle of the semi-dark hospital room. Letting me know that I didn't need to make an effort to speak, she kept me company until a nurse came by to announce the end of the visits. Had I not been able to survive the surgery, Kay would have been the last person I saw. Instead, I woke up from the surgery to find a confusing new set of rules that I had to live by, due to a body unable to make sense of processes that a day before seemed simply normal. I had a difficult path ahead of me. I'm 5 feet 11 inches tall, and I was 103 pounds when I left the hospital. Kay insisted that I move into her home at least until I was able to walk on my own, and able to experience some sense of independence and control.
>
> I did, and so did my sister who arrived from London shortly after to take care of me. As Kay always does with all of her guests, she created a welcoming environment for both my sister and me, and welcomed any change in the dynamics around the house in order to enable a support system for my recovery process. Only true friendship, the kind that overcomes cultural backgrounds, age, religious and political beliefs, can produce such an unselfish series of gestures.

Middle East Peace Camp

"It's a wonderful opportunity for young people to start appreciating other people and not to get into the mindset of being suspicious of strangers," Kay told *Seattle Post-Intelligencer* reporter Brad Wong. "All the religions honor strangers and encourage kindness to others."

This was the same Kay Bullitt who as a young woman had gone to postwar Germany, the same woman who had gone to Palestine with the Rev. Cabell Tennis, the same person still working for, searching for peace, this time after the horrible attacks in New York and Washington and in the sky over Pennsylvania on September 11, 2001. "I heard the appalling news on the radio," Kay remembers. She regularly tunes in to KUOW, the local National Public Radio station in Seattle. The event only added importance to Kay's next project.

Kay had attended an awards ceremony and met Maha Gebara and Susan Davis. They discussed the idea for a peace camp for children, based upon Gandhi's idea that "if we are to have real peace, we must begin with the children." Kay, who had sponsored camps in the '60s at 1125, said they could hold the camp in her yard. Davis and Gebara became its co-directors.

Several people interviewed for this book have chosen the word "convener" to describe Kay Bullitt. A motto of Kay's might well be what she means when she says, "When you bring people together around a purpose, good things happen." Susan Davis makes this point as well as anyone:

> By Susan Davis to the southendseattle.com website
>
> A month after 9/11, I was sitting in long-time Seattle civic activist Kay Bullitt's living room for a Middle East dialogue

with other concerned folks. We expressed anger, concern, fears, and action plans.

As a progressive Jew, I wondered what I could do that involved children, not because they should carry the burden of cleaning up the world we gave them, but rather, because they are a natural social investment that easily brings teens and adults together.

By early April, a group of mothers met to plan a summer program to bring Arab, Jewish, and other children together. We imagined a new "normal": growing up with the "other" and breaking down the barriers that make the "other" a monster. By knowing each other, we would create a place to see the humanity in each. Our children would not be able to hide behind ignorance as many of us had.

In July 2002, we held a one-week day camp in Kay's spacious yard. It was thrilling to see the number who joined us as counselors, project leaders and volunteers. We were also anxious about hate mongers. The police were notified; the media was cautioned: no coverage until camp is over. The campers and counselors were our responsibility and we worried about their safety.

That week was more than I could have imagined. Camp was jammed with activities to include all the interested adults and teens. The children played soccer, gymnastics, and volleyball. White canopies dotted the yard for arts and crafts, board games, science, storytelling, dance, cooking, cultural sharing, music, peace cities, henna and hospitality. Camp began and ended with circle time — a chance to reflect on the day.

We didn't think about what would come next, but as the week was coming to an end the campers and the counselors did and were already planning for year two. The organizing mothers hadn't thought beyond the first year, but we were eager to come back.

The Middle East Peace Camp brought kids together for games and learning from a variety of backgrounds and traditions: Arab Christians, Muslims, Arab-Americans, Jewish Americans and Israelis from throughout the Puget Sound area. The camp became a big success, so big that by 2007 it had outgrown 1125 and was moved to the UW for the following year.

Politics, more and less

Former Texas Gov. Ann Richards — she of the famous "He was born with a silver foot in his mouth" line — visited 1125. Kay hosted her for a fundraiser to collect money for Democratic candidates for the state Senate. The last Democrat to win the governor's chair in the Lone Star State, Richards could enflame the passions of liberal Democrats — and drew cheers for her silver-foot line referring to President George H.W. Bush delivered at the Democratic National Convention in '92. Out of office did not mean out of Democratic minds and hearts, and a good crowd whooped it up when she came calling in Seattle. Even so, it was not quite the same as the fervor of the faithful that trademarked the Lowry shrimp feeds.

The *Post-Intelligencer*'s Joel Connelly captured this in a lament — about the disappearance of the annual event — he wrote and published in August 2004:

> "… the Shrimp Feed was once an institution in local politics.
>
> It was reasonably priced, had volunteer help — a Sierra Club nabob cooked the shrimp, bartenders from gay taverns served the beer — and regularly drew 1,000 Democrats to Kay Bullitt's lawn on Capitol Hill.
>
> A highlight was arm-waving oratory by Congressman (later Governor) Mike Lowry. He would decry the Reagan administration's "insane" Star Wars policy, the "idiotic"

nuclear arms race, and conclude by pointing skyward and then downward toward the fires of hell, and cry, "We're right, and they're wrong!"

Lowry, as a private citizen, stayed involved. Among his interests was the peace movement, still a topic high on Kay's agenda. "The 'Wage Peace' sign in her driveway signals her interest in bridging conflict," wrote *P-I* reporter Debra Carlton Harrell in February 2006. "She still remembers joining international efforts to help traumatized children in postwar Germany." Harrell said more in the story, which was encouraging readers to nominate worthy citizen-activists for a Jefferson Award. It carried the headline:

Jefferson Awards: Winner of 1983 award still trying to bridge conflicts

Kay Bullitt hasn't rested in retirement

Her Capitol Hill home of 50 years contains artifacts from world travels, many with her husband and civic leader, Stimson Bullitt. It has been host to local gatherings, from Democratic fund-raisers to summer youth camps bridging understanding between divided groups — blacks and whites in the 1960s, and now, Jewish and Arab students.

She is still helping. Bullitt supports green building and other environmental causes through the family's private non-profit Bullitt Foundation.

Albeit ungentlemanly to refer to a woman's age, Kay had passed her 81st birthday and maintained a schedule and pace that many a generation younger could not, or would not, sustain. Kay's activities kept her busy pursuing her interests, personal and civic. She took special delight in the growth of her grandsons, Ben and Conrad.

Ben's artwork, Conrad's singing, frequently at the Sunday brunches. Despite their divorces, Andrew Schmechel, Jim Hailey (who had remarried and had a son) and their families were welcome too. Stim came even though he had remarried. Friends were free to stop by. And Kay herself would call on them. Jean Walkinshaw remarks that Kay often stops by her home and drops off a flower; sometimes it's in the morning when Kay is walking back from her exercise class. Attending concerts, lectures, dinner parties, political meetings — these all combined to fill out her calendar. Referring to Kay as being "retired" really did not apply.

Picnic No. 50

This year, 2008, the picnics in July would be very special as everyone wanted to celebrate their 50th consecutive year at 1125. In remembrance, Daniel Block spoke for many in recalling what the gatherings had meant to him:

> The Wednesday picnics were a regular part of my life while growing up in Seattle. In summer it was a midweek appointment for the family. Kay always had watermelon, popsicles, and coffee.
>
> The picnics were attended by a core of regulars and many others, 20 or 30 people on a quiet evening, 60 or 70 when it was busy. Everyone would bring a hamper but, if one came straight to the picnic without, there was always lots of food and good company. My father, Robert Block, had a table reserved on the deck outside the kitchen, and loved holding court there. For us kids it was a time to get together and play, (I liked the swing on the big tree). We also played croquet. For our parents it was a time to share their dreams and projects, with their friends, talk politics and how to make Seattle a better place.

Chip Ragen and his family moved to Federal Avenue East on Capitol Hill in the '60s when banks were redlining the area. His father was told not to move there because "the blacks were moving in." That was of no concern to the Ragens, who moved in anyway. Chip loved the picnics. He tells of the shenanigans they pulled: raiding neighbors' fruit trees, teasing Dorothy's pet raccoon, Lucy, until Lucy had enough of it and would spit back at them. Protective Dorothy would chase them off. Ben and Conrad remember distributing plates of watermelon slices and passing out ice cream bars. As grandsons they shared in Kay's hosting duties.

The picnics had drawn the attention of *The Seattle Times* three years earlier. Reporter Paula Bock wrote a piece for the paper's Sunday magazine. Said Kay to reporter Bock:

> Everyone feels comfortable coming to a picnic. Every year, we have people from all over. Last week, someone brought someone from Yugoslavia. People bring their own food. I provide watermelon, popsicles, ice cream bars and coffee. Last night we had 250 people. If I had to feed everyone, I don't think it would have lasted 47 years!

From across the street, neighbors Jeffrey and Susan Bland felt very welcomed when they moved in and were invited to join in the picnic fun. "Kay makes you feel so much a part of the family," Jeffrey Bland said. "Our first time there was like we'd been going for years."

Jean Walkinshaw, among some of the most long-standing 1125 picnic attendees, marvels that now "three generations of friends show up." It is the same for the Ragens and others. Kenan Block says he still goes if he is in town in July.

"There are only a very small number of people in the entire United States," observes neighbor Bland, "who would open up their grounds for a neighborhood picnic. It speaks to who Kay is and what she is about."

Dog park

No, 1125 had not become a place to park one's canine pal as when people park there cars at a garage. Woman's, or man's, best friend may have the off-leash run of the place, however, with owner or caretaker mindfully watching nearby. Kay had added a new activity to her yard. Neighbors could bring their dogs to romp around but "I limited the number to no

more than four at any one time," Kay says. Often, Kay's Zane (a golden retriever) and daughter Margaret's Emmett (a special mix) host their canine comrades. It's just one more way 1125 serves the community.

Death with dignity

"'I call it "death with dignity,"' said Kay Bullitt, 84, the venerable Seattle civic activist who had come to the dock to bid goodbye to the *Wawona*." Kay was quoted by *Seattle Times* writer Eric Lacitis, who, in effect, was writing an obituary:

> In 1963, after reading an article in this paper about the
> *Wawona* — then already deteriorating — Bullitt began the
> effort to save the ship.
> Since then, 46 years have gone by, with thousands of
> volunteer hours and numerous fundraising efforts. The ship,

in 1970, was the first vessel to be placed on the National Register of Historic Places. In 1977, the *Wawona* was designated an official Seattle landmark.

For Kay, the *Wawona* project had been the beginning, but its demise was not the end, but only one part, of the drive to preserve Seattle's maritime heritage and that of the Pacific Northwest. Since helping to organize Save Our Ships (SOS) in 1964, the effort to save the three-masted schooner *Wawona* bore fruit in other respects. SOS quickly became the nonprofit Northwest Seaport–Maritime Heritage Center. Over the years it managed to save three vessels. Its small fleet resides at the south end of Lake Union and marries up well with the glistening new Museum of History & Industry in the renovated former U.S. Naval Reserve Training Center.

The *Arthur Foss*, built in 1889; the *Swiftsure* lightship, built in 1904; and the fishing trawler *Twilight*, built in 1933, compose the inventory to date. For decades the Foss family here operated a large and successful tugboat business. The *Arthur Foss* was named for the company's founder, and when it retired from service, the family donated the boat to Northwest Seaport. Back in the 1930s, the *Arthur Foss* earned a movie credit when scenes of the tugboat race for the Metro-Goldwyn-Mayer film *Tugboat Annie* were shot on Elliott Bay. The *Swiftsure* was a U.S. Coast Guard ship that spent six-month tours at a specific location out on the ocean to provide navigation and weather information for ships at sea and for data collection for official record keeping. The *Twilight* was built in Seattle by H.C. Hansen and trolled for fish into the 1980s.

Valiant efforts to save other ships and boats came for naught. Seattle attorney Joe Shickich served as president of Northwest

Slowly and inexorably, the de-masted *Wawona* is towed to its deconstruction on Lake Union. Photo by Courtney Blethen, *The Seattle Times*.

Seaport for seven years and became involved, initially, by doing some pro bono legal work at Kay's request on the former Washington state ferry *San Mateo*. The effort to save the vessel for the collection did not succeed. But Shickich, at the Seattle firm of Riddell Williams, "felt honored that she had asked me to get involved." He stayed on and served as president of Northwest Seaport until 2009. "It's really been worthwhile," he says recounting the progress Northwest Seaport has made.

Hours of work, dozens of fundraisers, fidelity to the cause from her loyal adherents devoted to saving the *Wawona* could not keep pace with the cost to renovate her deteriorating wooden hull, bought initially for $27,000. The estimate to repair her back then was $75,000, according to Lacitis' article that appeared on March 9, 2009. In 1977 *Wawona* achieved status as a Seattle landmark. Sadly, however, Lacitis reported that

> By 2005, because of water intrusion that was followed by beetle infestation, a full restoration was estimated at $15 million.
>
> And so, said Joe Shickich, president of NW Seaport, the nonprofit that owns the *Wawona*, the decision was made to demolish her, with portions saved, such as the captain's cabin.

The saved portions will be featured in the new Museum of History & Industry going in at South Lake Union Park.

"It's a bittersweet day, a melancholic day," said Shickich, who was in another boat, following the *Wawona* to her end. "She's moving to the next stage."

An important part of that next stage was the salvaging of portions of the *Wawona*. Her steering mechanism was found to be in good condition. Shickich said it was carefully removed and sent to be transplanted in the *C.A. Thayer*, an identical twin to the *Wawona*, and part of the San Francisco Maritime National Historical Park at Fisherman's Wharf.

TOP: Grandparents for Obama organizer Susan Godfrey drew 25 people together at the Capitol Hill home of Kay Bullitt in Seattle to write personal postcards to undecided independent seniors in the battleground state of Florida.

BOTTOM: Friends watch the 2008 election returns as Barack Obama wins election as president of the United States.

RIP—*Seattle Post-Intelligencer*

Since 1863, long before Washington was admitted to the Union in 1889, the *Seattle Post-Intelligencer* covered news and developments as "The Voice of the Northwest." Now, on March 17, 2009, the last edition of the *P-I* would come off the presses. Long the dominant paper in Seattle, the *P-I* had been purchased by Hearst Newspapers in 1921. It began to lose its dominance in the mid-'50s. By the '70s, the *P-I* was losing money, despite its morning position. In 1983, in order to cut costs but continue publishing, the *P-I* and *Times* formed a joint operating agreement under the federal Newspaper Preservation Act.

The agreement meant *The Times'* management would run the business side of both papers (printing, advertising, circulation) but the two papers would retain separate ownerships and editorial voices. They would divide earnings, roughly two-thirds to the *Times*, one-third to the *P-I*.

The rise of the Internet, killing off lucrative classified advertising and offering free, if truncated, news coverage online, coupled with a new generation of people who did not read newspapers as had their parents, caused newspapers everywhere in the U.S. to lose revenues. Major cutbacks affected virtually every newspaper. Many shut down. That was the fate of the *P-I*. It would continue as an online newspaper. Effectively, however, Seattle became a one-newspaper town.

The *P-I* had become the Avis of Seattle's two daily newspapers: "We may be number two but we try harder." Well written, well edited and well regarded, the *P-I* stressed strong political coverage, strong features with an unmatched team of award-winning music and arts critics, at times a sassy attitude and an editorial voice moderately left of center. Its editorial cartoonist David Horsey earned two Pulitzer Prizes for best work. All this proved not to be enough.

Kay Bullitt speaks for thousands when she says: "I miss the *P-I*."

A complicated man

Charles Stimson Bullitt left this world April 19, 2009, leaving behind an astonishing legacy. The fact that he was a complicated man, at times a very difficult man, could not detract from his life, a life of remarkable achievement. A large gathering at Seattle's Town Hall marked his passing.

While he demanded much from others, he demanded more of himself. To do less seemed to him a cop-out. He was painfully shy, constantly feeling inadequate, and at times he could be cruel.

Post-Intelligencer writer Joel Connelly, who hiked and climbed with Stim, thoughtfully addressed Bullitt's personality:

> Stim was like a fine cognac. When you hold a snifter of cognac in your hands at first it is cold. But then it begins to warm up and release its complex flavors and aromas. Stim was like cognac. Among his friends, he might start out off to the side, and silent. Slowly, he would warm to the occasion and become quite the raconteur.

David Brewster, whom Stim hired for the staff at *Seattle* magazine and who got to know him over the years, observed that "Stim couldn't see in front of his nose but he could see around the corner." That says a lot and is said in respect for Stim as a visionary, for his strengths and weaknesses.

On the other hand, another admirer, Jean Walkinshaw, remembers that "he was caustic to Kay. But I guess he was that way with many people." Walkinshaw knew Stim and Kay well from the early days. Her late husband, Walt, had grown up with Stim. They practiced law together. Their families lived in the same neighborhood, played together on excursions here and there, and were close friends. "Still," Walkinshaw says, "he was brilliant."

Not enough credit has been given to Stimson Bullitt for the good works he did while head of King Broadcasting. Nor is his devotion to the outdoors, well known beyond the community of rock and mountain climbers. Yes, King Broadcasting lost money under his time as president. But thanks to his vision, King Broadcasting entered early on into the cable television business which over time proved to earn the company a financial bonanza. *Seattle* magazine lost money and folded at the end of the '60s. Importantly, it set a new, higher standard for journalism in Seattle that elevated the news coverage of the newspapers and other broadcast organizations — just as one outstanding superstar athlete will elevate the performance of the players around her.

Seattle magazine's editors and writers took on tough and controversial issues in a way the newspapers had not. The magazine expected and got very good writing from its reporters and editors. They delivered. As the decade wound down, *Seattle* magazine reporters teamed up with their counterparts at the *Post-Intelligencer* to conduct an investigation into what they proved to be a police payoff scandal. Their reports ended the career of police officials and King County Prosecutor and Republican kingpin Charles O. Carroll, and led to the election of new, more progressive political leaders.

Under Stim's presidency, King's Channel 5 in Seattle retained a first-rate news staff that included a focus on the tough subjects of race relations, better schools and holding elected officials accountable. Stim hired ethnic minority women for work on-air. One result was that the day-in, day-out news reporting at KING set the pace for broadcast journalism in town. Eventually, this affected how *The Seattle Times* and *P-I* covered the news as well. It is no stretch to say that Stim's tenure at the head of King Broadcasting set in motion forces that elevated the quality of journalism in Seattle.

The effect on the *P-I* was salutary. Under the leadership of such editors as Charles Dunsire, Ruth Howell and Jack de Yonge, the newspaper's editorial voice spoke up for progressive issues and more liberal political leaders. By the 1988 presidential campaign, *The Seattle Times* shocked the community by endorsing a Democrat for president, Gov. Michael Dukakis of Massachusetts.

Bullitt's *Seattle* magazine spawned another positive result. Following the magazine's demise, David Brewster became managing editor of *Argus*, a long-standing Seattle weekly newspaper published by the aging, sharp-tongued, but moderate Republican Philip Bailey. When Bailey retired and shut down the paper, Brewster started a new publication in 1976, *The Weekly*. In the run-up to that venture, Stim "helped in a small way and provided some support," says Brewster, who hired Patrick Douglas, formerly of the *Seattle* magazine staff, as *The Weekly's* first managing editor. "We did what we could to carry on some of the things we started at the magazine," said Brewster. He would successfully publish *The Weekly* for 21 years.

Stim's vision for improving downtown Seattle lives on today in the transformative success of Harbor Steps. It was hard. Dorothy had worked for seven years at Harbor Properties, serving as chief operating officer. During that time she managed a large portfolio: the properties, ski areas, video cable and mortgage companies.

Though she supported the plans to redevelop run-down First Avenue, Dorothy regarded as too risky Stim's plan to construct two apartment buildings on either side of a new stairway, Harbor Steps, from First Avenue leading down to Western Avenue and the waterfront. As a result of this conflict, Stim wound up firing her in 1992. That led to an estrangement.

Still, there were ample grounds for this breach to heal up. For one thing, Dorothy loved and admired her father. He felt the same about her. For another, it was Dorothy who had helped him overcome one of the demons he had carried much of his professional life. The story is worth telling, in Dorothy's words, by flashing back four years:

> In 1988, as I neared my Executive MBA (Master of Business Administration) graduation, it occurred to me that there were people in my class about to obtain MBAs from the UW who had never earned a college degree. This made me reflect on my father, who had always regretted his lack of degrees. He left Yale for World War II before he was able to complete college. Later, after the war, the UW Law School conditionally admitted him, permitting my father to take a full course load and sit for the bar. But he was not allowed an LLB because he lacked the prerequisite college degree. The lack of a degree proved a source of shame for decades and an impetus to be a lifelong learner.
>
> So I made a confidential appointment with the then dean of the UW's Law School. I asked if the school had ever graduated a law student who lacked a college degree. It had. With that precedent I asked the school to undertake a blind review of my father's 40-year-old transcript. I asked for a blind review because I wanted no special treatment of my distinguished father. If they determined he had earned a law degree on the merits and issued a diploma, that would, I

believe, have great meaning to him. Not so if the degree came in some honorary form.

So the law school and the UW administration undertook a comprehensive *blind* review of my father's transcript and determined that he did in fact deserve a degree on the merits of his academic work. They issued a diploma for a J.D. in 1988. With it they gave me a letter explaining their process. The next day I took the letter and framed diploma to my father's office. He choked up, then hooked the diploma to his wall. He promptly amended his résumé and reported his degree from that point forward whenever he gave a speech or received an award, etc.

For two years, Dorothy reflected and considered how best to heal the rift with her dad. She hit upon an idea for his 75th birthday. She put pen to paper and started to build a list of 75 happy memories they had shared over the years. With help from friend and fellow attorney Jim Wickwire — a celebrated climber and close friend of Stim's — Dorothy got her list packaged in handsome book form and delivered it to him the day before his birthday at his law firm office, Riddell Williams. Stim was moved heartily and called Dorothy in the next day. The division between father and daughter happily became history.

The fracture between Dorothy and Stim affected Kay. She cared and worried about the split between the two and stepped up for both. As Dorothy remembers, her mother "was steadfast in her support for me during that devastating time. Simultaneously she extended herself to Stim, keeping our extended family together for the long term."

No remembrance of Stim Bullitt would be complete or fair without a note on his love and devotion to the outdoors. The

From left: Bill Sumner, Stim and Jim Wickwire at 14,000 feet on Mt. McKinley, May 1978. Photo courtesy of Jim Wickwire.

Bullitt Foundation's support and advocacy for protecting the natural environment is one part his legacy — shared by other family members, including Kay. Another and major part of his life was regular engagement with that environment. He was an active outdoorsman, an elite rock climber and an avid mountain climber. Testimony to the latter comes from no less than Jim Wickwire, who ranks among the world's elite high-alpine climbers of the 20th century. A friend who made several climbs with Stim, Wickwire has conquered Mount Everest, K2, McKinley, Rainier plus a long list of others. With co-author Dorothy Bullitt, he told of his adventures and misadventures in a stirring book, *Addicted to Danger*, they published in 1999. Wickwire told *The Mountain Zone* newsletter:

> Lawyer, author, Renaissance man, Stim Bullitt's commitment
> to the climbing life is remarkable. I'll never forget our two
> expeditions together to Mt. McKinley, the first in 1978 with

Bill Sumner, the second with Stim alone in 1980. We weren't successful in reaching the summit, but he was a marvelous companion. In the many stormbound tent days we had, our discussions ranged far and wide: literature, history, politics, music, culture, and sharing anecdotes about some of the amazing people we'd encountered over the years.

Despite his acute disappointment from our two attempts, Stim was not to be denied the summit of McKinley. He went back a third time in 1981; he was successful with Sumner and Shelby Scates. At the time Stim was 62.

My most vivid memories of Stim, though, have been following him up a few short rock climbs in recent years. Here he was, twenty years my senior, leading me up pitch after pitch. It was all I could do to follow him.

Stimson Bullitt was married three times — to Kay for 24 years. After their divorce, the two found a new kind of relationship, a new friendship. Friends and family alike say, "Kay is the most forgiving person," and that is reflected in the welcoming spirit that infuses all her relations. Two years after Stim had moved out of 1125, there were Stim and Kay, holding hands, at the dinner celebrating John Goldmark. Over the years, there was Stim, welcomed at 1125 for the Sunday brunches — at times his third wife, Tina Hollingsworth, came with him — and other family events and special occasions.

Even though Stim had at times been hard on his own children, he took great delight in his grandchildren. This he and Kay held in common. Says Dorothy: "Our parents evolved into a very different relationship by the end, almost like siblings."

The memorial service occurred a year later, at the Stimson and Bullitt plots at the Evergreen-Washelli Memorial Park in north Seattle, just off Aurora Avenue North. It was a small family gathering: Dorothy and Margaret, Ashley, Fred and Jill, grandchildren

Conrad, Walker and Emma, and son-in-law Andrew. Dorothy organized the event, but everyone helped plan its component parts.

The service featured a stone bench in honor of Stim. His ashes had not been returned to his children, but, along with Kay, they wanted to commemorate him in a loving and dignified way. A stone marker was added to remember Ben. They had been denied the opportunity to bury him as his remains never were found. Both the bench and stone marker were placed next to the grave of Mrs. Bullitt. Family members read a passage, offered a remembrance, sang and interpreted an original work of art. Kay in the position of matriarch was the last to speak, reading from St. Francis of Assisi.

Even though it rained that day, Dorothy remembers that "the woman I worked with at Washelli arranged for an awning. Afterwards we had a beautiful picnic. Ashley brought the linen and silver of our great-grandmother Harriet O. Stimson. Ashley's daughter, Emma, an accomplished chef, provided the food."

Bench and marker (lower right) commemorating, respectively, Stimson Bullitt and Benjamin Bullitt at Evergreen Washelli Memorial Park, July 2010.

Caregiving

Andrew Schmechel and Margaret had divorced in 2000, yet their parting did not exclude Andrew from family activities. For a period of several months following their separation, Margaret and sons Ben and Conrad moved into 1125 until they could find a place for themselves to live independently. By 2009, however, Andrew suffered from bile duct cancer and Kay invited him to come live at 1125, where he could have quality care and loving support and be readily accessible to his sons. In many instances of divorce, the collateral damage to family members can be severe. Even on the good days, divorces are hard on people. In the case of the Bullitts, however, the acceptance, the larger love and generosity Kay exhibited affected the people around her. Everyone benefited, most particularly Ben and Conrad.

For a while, Andrew was able to move about as he underwent treatment. Still, the disease progressed and inevitably he became confined to bed. Finally, too ill and requiring a higher level of care and attention, he moved to Bailey-Boushay House in Seattle's Madison Valley, a care facility originally founded by Thatcher Bailey, the son of *Argus* publisher Phil Bailey, to care for people living with AIDS. It was June 2011, and the school year was coming to a close.

Andrew had hoped to attend his gifted son's performance in the Roosevelt High School production of *Titanic*. He couldn't. He was too weak. But a friend recorded the musical and in that way, lying in his sick bed, Andrew could hear Conrad's voice. The show closed the day before he died. Margaret remembers Andrew had worried that Conrad would not graduate. Ten days later, his son crossed the stage and received his diploma.

Kay's devotion did not exclude her daughters. Her presence and attention helped both: Margaret, a single mother raising two boys, who worked in real estate to support them; and Dorothy, as she moved on from Harbor Properties to management consulting, service for a term as president of Seattle Rotary No. 4, then CEO of the Seattle-King County Habitat for Humanity affiliate and on to her senior lecturer and distinguished practitioner teaching post at the UW's Evans School of Public Affairs.

Extending the family

The losses of Stim and Andrew and the withdrawal of Jim Hailey subtracted some key family members from the Sunday brunches. In terms of Kay's extended family, however, a continuo of renewal brought new people into the fold, including Craig Jensen and Filippo Artoni, whom Dorothy regards as "my Italian nephew."

Artoni hails from Milan, and, as a foreign exchange student, lived at Margaret's home when Conrad was a senior at Roosevelt. According to Dorothy, "The next year he lived at Kay's (since he was 17, I served as his guardian) while he attended Seattle Central Community College. At 19 he is now a junior in pre-med at the UW. He attends Sunday brunch at Kay's nearly every week." Meanwhile, Jensen became an important actor at 1125 as well.

1125 gets a "tune-up"

By the 2000s, some 55 years' worth of Seattle's weather had taken a heavy toll on 1125's A-frame structure and systems. Water damage seeping through the unprotected windows on the west side led to some dry rot; the in-floor heating system no longer worked; issues with the plumbing and a litany of other problems added up to a run-down house.

Margaret had introduced Kay to Craig Jensen. Thanks to her son Conrad's participation in musical theater, which also involved Jensen, Margaret learned not only of Jensen's musical talent but also that he was quite expert in the practical arts of carpentry, plumbing — in fact, most of the things one needed to know to maintain a house in good condition. So when Jensen put on a reading at 1125 of the musical he had written, *Something Nasty in the Woodshed*, he came face to face with a building in need of some serious repair.

"We had a limited budget," Jensen recalls. Even so, along with his 80-year old father, Bob, Jensen developed a low-cost plan and set about restoring the awning over the west-side windows and second-floor deck that protected the house from the direct hits of wind and rain. Over the course of these initial repairs, Kay and Jensen became good friends.

A year later, Jensen moved in temporarily and learned firsthand of the problems and vagaries plaguing 1125. He set about a restoration project that took several months. With help from his father, who had taught him the skills of home maintenance and repair, Jensen repaired the water damage, replaced broken plumbing, rebuilt the second-floor balcony, devised an economical yet effective new heating system, and repaired and renovated other parts of the house that returned 1125 to its original glory but with one important difference. "I can now sit in my living room and be warm," declares Kay. "I could not do that before Bob fixed the heating."

"She is so welcoming, so interesting," Jensen says. "At her house, there is always something interesting going on. When that front door opens, you don't know who may come in but it will always be someone interesting."

South Pacific Islander students

They were small in number, the cohort of kids of the South Pacific Island culture, about 2,500 when the program to focus on their needs got under way. In the Seattle School District of about 47,000 students, they had fallen through the cracks.

Low performance, high dropout rates, low graduation rates and a variety of social problems left unattended caused Von Tresckow and Betty Patu to focus their attention on helping these kids succeed in school. Their efforts paid off. Now Betty was running for the Seattle School Board. Kay Bullitt sponsored a fundraiser at 1125 to help Betty win. It was August 4, 2009.

Kay had first met Von Tresckow when, as a veteran Seattle Public Schools teacher, he organized the South Pacific Islander Task Force. Kay served on the task force and quickly recognized the need to bring special help for these students. Her contacts at school district headquarters, and knowledge of educational issues here, "made her very instrumental in helping to push for attention to the South Pacific Islander students," Patu said. "She called the district out in several ways."

Kay says the South Pacific students came from a culture where, rather than sit in a seat all day and be talked at, they needed teachers trained to adapt to their style and culture. Betty Patu was asked to establish a program tailored for these students. "Our kids need to see pictures of what the teachers are talking about," Patu said. "They are very hands-on learners. We focused on bringing back the dropouts, starting with the primary level, then the middle and high school levels." The program succeeded so well that the school district added some funds to extend it. They opened it up to all students and it lasted 11 years.

Christmas 2010 at 1125—Back row:
Andrew, Conrad, Filippo Artoni, Stefan
Walker and Ben; front: Margaret, Dorothy,
Kay, Ashley, Emma, and (dog) Emmett.

Chapter 10

Activities by the tens

Kay, these days, is the great
family unifier. She is our center.
I imagine us all flying off into space,
like an expanding universe, when
she finally has to leave us.
— Jill Bullitt

In 2006, to *P-I* reporter Debra Carlton Harrell, Kay offered her
personal credo:

> "If you get on one path, you have to keep following it,"
> Bullitt says. "The trouble is, I have too many paths. But as I
> look back over my life, I've been consistent in my interests —
> education, civil rights, historic preservation, the environment,
> international understanding and peace and the arts. They are
> important social issues to me — and there's still a lot to do."

The meetings, the gatherings, the Sunday brunches, the fundraisers continue apace at 1125. The Opera Guild previews two operas at 1125. Donors pony up handsomely at fundraisers for Democrats Jay Inslee, campaigning successfully for governor, and Peter Goldmark, for re-election as state land commissioner. Peter Steinbrueck is running for mayor of Seattle and Kay holds a fundraiser for him too. He will lose out in the primary.

A new project led by Bob Walsh, Cold War Connections, is being conducted in conjunction with the Museum of History & Industry. It seeks to bring together people involved in citizen diplomacy from the Target Seattle-Goodwill Games days.

1125 "Hollywood North"

Writer and filmmaker Julio Ramirez had suffered, and painfully so, with Crohn's disease and managed, through several difficult surgeries, to survive.

He wrote a screenplay and directed a film about four individuals contemplating suicide and titled it *Nothing Against Life*. Locations for the filming included Volunteer Park, just five blocks east of Kay's house, and 1125 itself. As Ramirez remembers this project,

> Even more special to me was Kay's level of enthusiasm about the making of the film, and the involvement of our good mutual friend and Kay's longtime gardener, Lisa Durango. Aside from appearing in the film as part of the ensemble cast, Lisa helped us during different stages of pre-production and production, as well as coordinating the logistics while filming at Kay's house.
>
> We filmed in several areas of the garden and in the main social area of the house. We also took over the attic, where we had our wardrobe and hair and makeup departments, and

[took] over the basement, where we had our craft services and served our cast and crew meals. In addition, Kay's daughter, Dorothy Bullitt, served as executive producer for the film. Kay's grandson, Walker Schwartzman, also participated in the film as production assistant, and as a part of the ensemble cast.

Following the filming, Ramirez credits Ashley for playing "an active and important role during the post-production stage of the film." *Nothing Against Life* made its debut at an international film festival in Italy in 2013. Perhaps more important, Kay reports, Julio underwent successful chemotherapy and successfully fought off lymphoma. He has managed to soldier on, even though his case of Crohn's disease remains a problem.

There was a kind of symbolic bookend to 2013, one that reflected that first year that Kay arrived in Seattle. Work was well under way to tear down the Alaskan Way Viaduct and to replace it with a tunnel. The project would open up the city's magnificent waterfront, one that people would experience by climbing down Stim Bullitt's Harbor Steps. But unlike 1973, when she helped to plan it, Kay would not be involved in arranging the 2013 edition of Bumbershoot. The event would not only draw large crowds but also would enjoy a sunlit Labor Day weekend, bumbershoots not needed — thank you very much!

Lisa Durango

Kay's busy life is replete with examples where one project or activity leads to another, wherein she will meet someone who will introduce her to someone else and a new connection, and new endeavor, results. This happened at the Middle East Peace Camp

Kay inaugurated in 2002. "The first day of the camp, D'Vorah Kost came and said she had a gardener helping her with her yard and perhaps I would like to have her help out here," Kay says. "Well, my yard needed a lot of help then, so I was glad to have her come over. That's how I met Lisa Durango."

Lisa was so good at fixing up the gardens and grounds that soon Kay had her working full-time. Lisa had a dog named Zane, who was her constant companion. She had a family but they had evinced little interest in her. Lisa was not always in good health and had been in Swedish Hospital at Christmastime 2011 with serious lung problems. With work at Kay's and Kost's, she was managing quite well until she became ill.

"She had found an apartment in Lake City," Kay says. "She was so proud to be on her own." But one day after not hearing from or seeing Lisa, Kay's handyman Allistair went to her apartment and found her dead. This was a sad loss. Kay and Lisa had become very close friends. Kay sponsored a memorial for Lisa, held in her living room at 1125.

With Lisa gone, Kay needed not only a new gardener but also someone to help out at the house. She had met Claudia Arguero, who had worked for neighbor Marsha Rosellini (Victor's widow) until she moved from her nearby Capitol Hill home to the Mirabella, a community for seniors. Claudia had adopted Zane, and so when she moved into 1125 to be Kay's live-in companion, Zane came along too.

A Left-Wing Tea Party

The invitation from the Metropolitan Democrats read: "A Left-Wing Tea Party. At 2 p.m. Saturday, April 20, at the Mount Zion Baptist Church." Former Gov. Mike Lowry would present Kay with

METROPOLITAN DEMOCRATIC CLUB
of SEATTLE

invites you to a

Left-wing Tea Party

Saturday, April 20, 2:00 – 4:00 pm
Mt Zion Baptist Church, 1634 19th Ave, Seattle

In which

Gov Mike Lowry presents an
MDC Lifetime Achievement Award to
Kay Bullitt

and

THE MAD HATTER MEETS THE US TEA PARTY

$25 adults, $12.50 children under 10, $100 sponsorships
RSVP joanvlawson@gmail.com, 206-382-3147
Or pay at metrodems.org

the MDC Lifetime Achievement Award. The well-attended event went off as planned with one happy exception.

A group of women in another part of the building were busy making sandwiches for a homeless shelter. Among them was Elma Horton. Stepping down the hall, Elma heard the sounds of the MDC party, and as she passed by the open door, Lowry was heaping praise on Kay Bullitt. Elma could not resist.

She entered the room, walked up to the microphone next to Lowry and asked if she could say a word. Lowry gave her the floor, and Elma added her salute to Kay: telling the audience how her children had benefited from participating in Kay's integrated summer camps some 50 years ago. It was, to paraphrase the Bible — they were in a church, after all — a poignant example of the admonition that you reap what you sow.

Between 1953 and 2013, Seattle's political landscape changed so dramatically one can only speculate that those liberal Democrats may not even have dreamed it would turn so far in their direction. Former Gov. Mike Lowry described this change succinctly: "It used to be that for a Democrat to win a statewide office, he needed to carry at least 40 percent of the vote in King County. Now it's just the opposite, only for Republicans." There is no doubt, adds Lowry, "that those determined, committed liberals helped make that happen."

What goes around ...

Patrick Burr brought home another happy payback from the '70s. He was the young man who had been Dorothy's high school sweetheart, during those challenging years at Garfield High. Kay liked Patrick, and as they got to know one another back then, she

A hearty brunch at Kay's kitchen table: from left, Ashley Bullitt, Margaret Bullitt, Patrick Burr, Kay in foreground.

talked with him and counseled him in ways that a young man needs when trying to find his way. Despite the eventual parting of the teens, Patrick never forgot Kay and her genuine caring in his time of need.

Now, nearly 40 years later, he and Dorothy found each other. Despite the fact that he was terminally ill, they fell in love again and were together until his death. Before he died, however, he demonstrated his love for Kay. As Dorothy tells it:

> He never forgot and he adored her across the decades and was thrilled to be back in her home. One Sunday, despite his Stage IV prostate cancer and advanced heart disease, Patrick insisted on getting down on his hands and knees to refinish Kay's balcony floor, weathered from leaks. He wanted to do that for her. He also was an expert at cleaning her bacon grill each Sunday — having run a restaurant kitchen maintenance business.

Another happy birthday

Kay's affection for her family, her very large family, remains strong and consistent. Examples are many and varied, and yet they are really born of the same devotion. In June 2013, Kay hosted a yard party for Makaiya's birthday. In part the occasion also spotlighted Makaiya's graduation with honors from New York University.

> "She always welcomes me and my family to stay with her," says Jill. "Most recently, [June 2013] she put up Makaiya, David, me, and three of Makaiya's friends for a few days, and we had a beautiful graduation party for Makaiya in her yard. She then kept David on after, and took care of him, as he had come down with pneumonia on the trip."

Jill and David underwent a difficult divorce. Yet Kay stands firmly supportive of both: "I called David and told him I still consider him my son," Kay says with a smile." To Jill,

> Kay, these days, is the great family unifier. She is our center. I imagine us all flying off into space, like an expanding universe, when she finally has to leave us. I miss her tremendously and hate that my own path takes me so far away right now.

At summer's end, Jill accompanied Makaiya to Dublin, where her daughter will study American literature, a field of study inspired by her father, David. Following that, Makaiya plans to attend law school. Therefore, it is from a distance that Makaiya offers some affectionate thoughts about "Grandma Kay."

> She excels in the indescribably important acts of love: "forwarding" my gifts from Santa when I was younger; coming to all of my high school plays, flowers in hand; flying across the country for graduations and birthday parties; welcoming an endless litany of my friends and me for impromptu sleepovers; and — last but not least — even making my favorite blueberry pancakes during Sunday breakfast.
>
> And yet, still for me, my favorite memory is a particular one of us talking. It was one of those in-between times of day, maybe we were headed to the opera in a few hours, or maybe everyone else in the house was taking a nap, but everything seemed immobile to me just then, and, meanwhile, I was incensed by some statistic about the de facto inequality of American education.
>
> Today, I wince a bit at how sheltered I must have been, but 10 years ago, I was supremely in earnest as I confided my worries in Grandma Kay: people my age, who looked like me, and who I knew, even, were getting bad educations. Life

Family Photos

Melita and Prairie Rose

Melita and Crystal

Front, Fred, Mercedes, Melita; rear, Cyrena and Keeshawn

David, Makaiya and Jill, Dublin, 2014

Jill chats with guest at opening of her art exhibition in 2005.

In Kay's living room, grandchildren: Conrad, Walker, Stefan, Makaiya, Emma and Ben

Kay's grandchildren: Walker, Ben, Emma, Makaiya and Stefan gather in Port Townsend, Washington, to celebrate Stefan's high school graduation

Makaiya's graduation from Lakeside 2008: Back row, Stefan, David, Margaret, Kay, Ashley, Dorothy, Makaiya, Jill, Claude, front, Andrew and Conrad

Front from left: Dorothy, Margaret, Ben; back from left, Stim, Kay, Jill and cousin Jacque Collins (1960s)

wasn't fair ... and there I was, about to go to a private school.

Grandma Kay listened to my horror, with concentration enough to make me feel authentic, and responded with this: Apparently, a group of philanthropists near Chicago wanted to try busing good teachers into economically disadvantaged schools, instead of busing minority kids out. She was following the news coverage closely, because she thought it might prove a useful tactic in Washington state too.

That was the first time we had ever talked about current events, just the two of us. In doing so, Grandma Kay gave me something concrete to hold on to, a way to be both pragmatic and ideal-driven when it came to enacting change. More than a grandmother's ability to comfort her granddaughter, she offered me an alternative to being scared off by the ubiquitous injustice of the world. She talked me into agency; she was the first to fully explain to me the importance of action.

More was in play than celebrating Makaiya, and not to diminish that happy event. It speaks to Kay's vision, her ability to see, to grasp a larger reality and to deal with it. It speaks to her influence by example, its effects on others.

Makaiya's father, David, had arrived under the weather. Stress from the divorce, from moving, from meeting up again with Jill after months of separation and now a powerful cold left him looking wan. He made it through a family evening party but left early, on Kay's arm. By the next day, as the 1125 household prepared to receive friends for a picnic, David sat in the kitchen and, he says,

Evidently, I was starting to look as wan and enfeebled as I felt, for both Margaret and Jill asked me if I shouldn't call the doctor. I thought, well, this is not going to happen, not on the day of my daughter's great celebration. Finally, Margaret sat down beside me and said, "I would be glad to go with you to the emergency room." What moments before seemed extreme now seemed both plausible and finally desirable.

Margaret took David to the emergency room. X-rays revealed a clear case of pneumonia. Kay insisted that he stay at 1125, take the time needed to recuperate and heal up, the two in Kay's mind connected but not identical. David says,

> Used to independence, I found myself gratefully accepting the angelic ministrations of the house, Kay making many of my meals herself and urging Claudia to come up with soups and stews she thought were appropriate for the recovery. And it happened — I recovered, each day inching toward health, at first sleeping into the afternoon, then rising to sit in the yard and read and write undisturbed under the great elm that we feared the city of Seattle would one day ax. In the end, although adrift from the family, I didn't want to leave. Kay and I were having daily conversations about things of the world, as well as things of the heart. These extended also to Dorothy, who was, like her sister Margaret, quietly observant and solicitous. But the time to leave came.
>
> Some time after I had returned back East, I received a moving letter from Kay saying how deeply glad she was to be able to provide me with what I needed to recuperate. It was a letter of touching dignity and expressive beauty, promising me that, regardless of my marital status, I was and would always be a member of the family, in fact, her son. I momentarily saw myself, as in a vision, with Andrew and Peggy Rabb and with her own lost son, Ben. In my 64th year, that was something I needed to be said to me.

A social venture capitalist

Dorothy offers an observation about her mother that rings true, that captures the Kay Bullitt modus operandi: it is that Kay is a social venture capitalist, an entrepreneur who invests *herself* in people and their projects, in social terms, and because she believes in people and sees their potential. Money may or may not be part of her investment. Her special gift is caring, support, offering ideas and suggestions, helping them connect the dots of what they want and need to do, connecting the right people to launch a given venture.

Why this works so well is that Kay genuinely cares about people. So her investment always includes a large portion of herself. Seen in this light, expressed in the lexicon of the business world, the currency of social venture capitalism begins with human caring, empathy for others, a willingness to meet people on their terms, to learn about their needs and then to help them strive to reach their goals. In Lisa's case, she wanted to live independently on her own. Kay's "investment" by retaining her to work in the yard, and at the same time providing the opportunity to become friends, enabled Lisa to be on her own.

Two of the characteristics prominent in Kay's brand of social venture capitalism are her willingness to risk failure and her expectation to remain in the background. She will accept but not seek out credit. Her reward comes in others' success. These characteristics explain why Kay Bullitt, so early on, earned credibility with Seattle's African-American community. Because she genuinely believed in and would work for their interests, they, in turn, included her as a leader in their councils and projects. So it has been with other groups and individuals.

A wonderful, most personal tribute to Kay comes from her close, longtime friend, Jean Walkinshaw:

> Since Walt died [April 2010], Kay has been central to my feeling that life is worth living. Every other morning she stopped by for breakfast on her way up the hill from exercise, and seldom has a week gone by that she hasn't asked me over for a glass of our favorite wine. She is a *true* friend and so totally accepting of the foibles and shortcomings of others (including me). Now that I am seeing more of her, I am struck by her amazing energy and drive to contribute to society.

Walkinshaw adds, "She is not a goodie-goodie, though. She is fun and bends with the present. I have seen her gambling in Las Vegas with the best of them and loving it until she began to lose."

New mileposts

She saw promise and potential, even if she did not see the world headquarters of Starbucks occupying the old massive Sears Roebuck building. She saw openness even where there was not open housing; she sensed that fairness could be won because Seattle had a willingness to embrace change. She met and made new friends who drew her in to a community striving to be bigger, better and of benefit to people shoved to the periphery of society. She would work to open doors and create the means to bring these disenfranchised the opportunities and the means to enjoy better lives.

That city where a new airliner had been launched was the same one now launching an entirely new one made of composite materials. The Boeing Company no longer kept its headquarters in Seattle, but in Chicago. Yet, the new Seattle is now headquarters to one of the world's most important philanthropic foundations: the

Bill & Melinda Gates Foundation. The Gates family was a Seattle family. So well focused was the Gates Foundation that no less than the "Oracle of Omaha," Warren Buffett, pledged his own massive fortune to augment the Gates program. The fortune that infused the Gates Foundation with money had come from Microsoft, the company that Bill Gates and Paul Allen had invented, the company that helped in a big way to bring the Internet and technologies to use it into homes and businesses around the world. Allen and his family set up their own huge foundation to benefit society. Kay had used her resources to travel the world in the cause of peace, to advance education, to experience and to learn from other peoples in their own lands and habitats.

The 60th year of Kay Bullitt's life in Seattle marked the city as one of the best places for live theater in the United States. Its music scene included a wide range of sounds, and had been the onetime home of a rocker named Jimi Hendrix of Garfield High School, and a popular band called Nirvana. Globally, distinguished Seattle-based scientists now work in such promising fields as genetics, cancer treatments and pharmaceuticals. Nordstrom markets fashion, Amazon sells — everything — with the click of a button, Starbucks brews coffee and new ideas are brewing in the city that Kay's ideals helped to reinvent. Many changes had caused the maturation and sophistication of Seattle. Yet the city still faced daunting problems.

A short list includes homelessness, a wide gap in student performance in its (still underfunded!) public schools, severe tensions among police and some ethnic minority communities, too much street crime, a very high cost of living that makes Seattle housing expensive and transportation problems that stretch to the horizon

Kay makes the rounds to greet
picnickers at the last picnic of 2013.

of time and beyond the capacity to pay for their remedies. All told,
however, just as in 1953, when Kay Muller arrived in Seattle, new
waves of young people continue arriving in the city they too see as
one of promise.

2013 — The last picnic

This year Kay extended her Wednesday evening July picnics by one
week into August. Margaret Russell's schedule prevented her from
making the July evenings. Kay was not going to close out the season
without Margaret and her husband, Dennis, so she added one for
August 7.

The balmy weather is perfect! Right on schedule, Margaret and Dennis arrive. Already the yard begins to fill. Most of the tables are taken, so some folks lay out their blankets, spread out their victuals and open the wine, or beer, or iced tea and begin to socialize. There is a mix of old-timers, in some cases three generations' worth. Some are newcomers. A family with several teens has a soccer ball they kick around. A dad and his young daughter punch a volleyball back and forth over the net set up at the south end of the yard. A soft but audible buzz fills the warm evening air as the conversations grow with the arrival of more people.

Like any grandparent, Kay is enormously proud and close to her grandchildren. Conrad could not attend the picnic. He had been in Seattle for a visit. But the day before, he returned to school at Oklahoma City University to appear in the musical *9 to 5* and to rehearse for leading his role in Kurt Weill's opera *Street Scene*. His voice would have added to Margaret Russell's and is missed. Ben is there and represents the grandchildren. He is back in Seattle for a visit with his "wonderful grandmother." A graduate of Princeton, he will return to studies at the University of London and his room-mates, Ashley's two sons, Walker and Stefan. The three cousins live in East London. Stefan is studying art and design. He has, on occasion, worked as a runway model. Walker, who family members say more than anyone else in the clan looks like Stim Bullitt, is in graduate school at Mike Leigh's acclaimed London film school.

Like her brothers, Emma Schwartzman is an artist, of the culinary variety. She moved to Cork, Ireland, where, at Ballymaloe, she studied cooking and learned about foods from the ground up. Among her chores were milking a cow, making cheese, growing vegetables, cooking full meals and baking fresh breads — all fueled by drinking gallons of tea. In Seattle, foodies and gourmets alike may have tasted her creations while she cooked with noted chefs de cuisine Matt Dillon and Emily Crawford, or with Ethan Stowell. She also is famous for her floating hot dog stand, plying Lake Union or Lake Washington near the University of Washington.

Ashley is there too. Now that she lives near 1125 on Bellevue Avenue East, she and Kay have grown closer. Ashley stops by for visits, perhaps for some quiet moments in the yard, and on occasion to do her laundry. This evening Ashley chats with family and friends at the picnic, an independent spirit puffing away on cigarettes — Kay's no-smoking policy notwithstanding.

By 7 p.m. the sun slips low in the sky, sending a glow back over Harvard Avenue East. The picnic is in full swing. Kay personally visits the tables, greeting individuals and clusters of folks, some rising to give her a hug. She pauses to chat longer with some. People approach her to catch her up on their doings. Soon, Ben circulates amid the tables and blankets of picnickers passing around the plates of watermelon slices and ice cream bars.

About 8:30, Margaret Russell picks up her guitar, heads into the house, sits down on the ledge in front of the fireplace and consults with the people gathering around as to what songs they should sing. Moments later, the sing-along is under way. Outside, the conversations continue softly as the evening's light fades away. But on Kay's face, the expression of delight glows as bright as ever.

Margaret Russell, with guitar (upper right),
leads the traditional sing-along that concludes
Kay's 2013 series of summer picnics.

Kay Muller Bullitt, 2013.

Afterword

Tuesday morning at 7 a.m. will find Kay doing exercises at the Montlake Community Center. Back home, she reads both *The Seattle Times* and *The New York Times*, regularly. Her 10 a.m. meeting has been canceled, so her morning

will be free until lunch, out with a friend. If she is not working on a particular project, she may sit down and continue reading her latest book, *Plutonia* by Kate Brown. Its subtitle indicates it is about "Nuclear Families, Atomic Cities and the Great Soviet and American Plutonium Disasters." "It is fascinating," Kay declares.

Almost every day, Kay and her sister Margaret Baillie chat by phone. Both are in their 80s, they are close and keep each other up to date on their respective community activities. A slower step does not deter Kay from taking walks with friends. She likes the stairs at 1125 leading up to the balcony. "Good for my legs," she says.

At 4 p.m. Wednesday, 1125 will host Pacific Northwest Connections, bringing together people from the former Soviet Union. On a different Wednesday, there will be an evening meeting for a group of about 12 to gather for the One World Now Project. They are recently returned from Morocco. They will discuss the trip and plans for teaching Arabic and Chinese to juniors in high school. On yet another evening, about 40 people will come for music by City Cantabile.

Thursday, she has visits from friends coming — one at 10 a.m., the other at 2 p.m. The phone rings a lot; perhaps it's Margaret or Dorothy checking in. Friends and colleagues working on projects stay in regular touch. Kay well may answer the call with "I'm in a meeting, I'll call you back."

Friday's schedule begins with morning exercise class, a doctor's appointment at 9 a.m., then lunch at home. Claudia is an excellent cook and makes marvelous homemade soups and fresh salads, among other delectables. An afternoon ride on "The Duck" will find Kay bundled up and out in the rainy and breezy weather for a tour of the city, including a cruise on the lakes.

Once a month on Saturdays, an architectural tour will stop in to study and admire 1125. Tomorrow is Sunday-brunch day, a highlight of Kay's week. That means last-minute arrangements on Saturday, ensuring the right provisions are on hand.

Sunday morning, Ashley and Dorothy come early to help with preparations. Soon other family and extended-family members arrive. To be sure, there is plenty to talk about at Kay

Bullitt's: social issues, politics, art exhibits or performances, individual projects, family members away at school, starting new jobs and gossip.

Zane, Emmett and Dorothy's collie, Teddy, conduct their own socializing out in the yard. Inside, folks will enjoy music, either someone performing or singing, or both. They may play Bananagrams — using tiles like in Scrabble to form words. By mid-afternoon, people start to leave. When there is a performance, Kay and Harriet will attend a Sunday matinee at Seattle Opera. They are longtime season ticket holders.

If staying home, as Kay does most Sundays, often Margaret will read aloud to her. "She is an excellent reader," says Kay. Currently, Margaret is reading *Moby Dick*. The next book Margaret may read is *War and Peace*.

Acknowledgments

Obvious as it is, this book could not, would not have been completed without the generous help and guidance of Kay Bullitt and her marvelous daughters. Their patience with me, my picky emails asking for information — some they already had given to me — I am sure stretched their generosity and forbearance.

Portions of their lives are not easy to discuss, especially with a stranger who is charged to write about them. They did not flinch. They took the time to provide details, some most private, without which my understanding would be insufficient to the task. Their help made all the difference. These women are — to employ the vernacular — awesome!

During an all too brief meeting in Portland with Fred Nemo, I found myself in the company not only of a brilliant man, but someone who cares deeply about his family and the foibles of the human condition. Fred's willingness to share his insights helped to provide warp and weft to this story. No less is that true for Fred's sister Jill. At a busy and difficult time in her life, she made time to provide comments and reflections that added significantly to my grasp of her story, as it fits into the larger fabric of *1125*.

Of course any and all deficiencies in the way I have related the stories throughout this work are mine alone. Surely there are instances where readers will find specific facts or descriptions that fall short of their memory or understanding, or what they conveyed to me. One of the challenges the writer faced was that people may remember the same event, or person, or who did what, but remember it differently from someone else. My attempts to resolve those differences I hope do not add to any confusion that may exist.

There are no exceptions to the rule — well, Mozart is one — that every writer needs an editor. Good fortune made the estimable Barbara "Bobbie" Stenson available and willing to serve as editor and publishing manager for *1125*. Her experience as a journalist, her work in government and historic preservation, rendered her an ideal professional to review the manuscript. She made this product better.

I must express my high regard and deep appreciation to my former colleagues for their generous help as this project got under way: Joel Connelly, the last of Seattle's great political writers, at seattlepi.com; David Brewster, thoughtful observer and incisive writer, founder of *The Weekly*, Town Hall and online news organization Crosscut; and Richard Campbell, the *P-I*'s unequaled former music critic, whose new book on Allied Arts is an important contribution to the history of our community. These men shared with me their knowledge and insights that helped illuminate my understanding of the period and people about which I have written.

To all those reporters whose news articles are referenced in the text, I thank them. Their work allowed me to nail down dates and details I would not have on my own been able to access. Just as critical to this project were several others. Carolyn Marr, archivist at the Museum of History & Industry cheerfully helped locate pictures from the *Post-Intelligencer* photo archive, which has resided at MOHAI since the print version of the *P-I* shut down in 2009. She is a gem of a researcher and a marvelous resource for people interested in learning more about our history. One must also acknowledge the helpful assistance of a half-dozen librarians at the Main Branch of the Seattle Public Library. While not named here, these devoted public servants helped me with a variety of tasks done in the course of gathering information about the people and events described herein. Finally, the website HistoryLink.org, founded by the late Walt Crowley, is a terrific resource and helpmate to anyone probing Washington state's history and the people who made it. I relied upon it constantly during the research and writing of *1125*.

Assembling photographs, locating news clippings for possible reproduction, even taking some new pictures, proved to be a much larger challenge than one initially thought. Faustino Lopez at Perfect Copy and Print on Broadway cheerfully helped facilitate this aspect of the project. Smart, patient and always ready to help, Faustino carefully calibrated the contrast and sizing to produce the best results when scanning in the art. This is not an easy task as some older materials, particularly from the newspapers, were difficult to copy, even using top-of-the-line equipment.

Finally, the many people interviewed for this book get my sincerest thanks. Each one eagerly took time to relate their experiences working with Kay. Without exception, each one spoke admiringly of her genuine caring for others; dedication to the cause of fairness, justice and peace among peoples; and how hard she has strived to make our community a better place. Among this cohort, I must spotlight Jean Walkinshaw and Anne Stadler. Interestingly both are distinguished television producers with a keen eye for people and events. Their insights helped me immensely to appreciate the depth and dimension of the peace movement, here and abroad, and of Kay's enduring commitment to it.

Kay Bullitt — honors and awards

A Jefferson Award for Public Service

The YMCA Milnor Roberts Award for World Peace Through International Understanding

The Partners in Public Education (PIPE) Katharine Muller Bullitt Award (named for its founder)

The Ralph Bunche Award from the Peace Through Law Section of the Seattle Bar Association

The Paul Beeson Award from the Washington Physicians for Social Responsibility

The First Citizen Award of 2000, sponsored annually by the Seattle-King County Association of Realtors — given to five members of the Bullitt family

The United Nations (Seattle Chapter) **Human Rights Award**

The Metropolitan Democratic Club Lifetime Achievement Award

Senior Services 2013 Lifetime Achievement Award

Further readings

Addicted to Danger, by Jim Wickwire and Dorothy Bullitt. Simon and Schuster (Pocket Books) 1998

Filling the Void, by Dorothy Bullitt. Simon and Schuster (Rawson Associates) 1996

River Dark and Bright—A Memoir, by Stimson Bullitt. Willows Press, 1995

To Be a Politician, by Stimson Bullitt. 1994 paperback edition

We Tried to Do Everything: Allied Arts in the Civic Landscape, by Richard Campbell

See *The Weekly*, April 13-April 19, 1983, "Citizens of Tashkent, Arise," available at the Seattle Public Library, main branch in downtown Seattle

Index

Numbers listed in italic refer to photographs.

About the author

Sam R. Sperry lives in Seattle. His career in
journalism and government includes reporting
for *The Seattle Times* and writing for the
editorial pages of the *Seattle Post-Intelligencer*.
He managed the Seattle Energy office under
Mayors Wes Uhlman and Charles Royer,
served as press officer for King County
Executive Randy Revelle and, briefly, as policy
director for Gov. Gary Locke. He taught
political science part-time at Seattle University
and worked in public affairs consulting for
Gogerty-Marriott. His volunteer activities
include Habitat for Humanity and the
St. Vincent de Paul Society. He and his wife,
Winnie, have four grown children and seven
grandchildren.